TAIPEI CITY
TAIWAN
TRAVEL GUIDE

**A Modern Explorer's Guide to Taipei:
Where Tradition Meets Innovation**

NICHOLAS Z. ANDREW

TABLE OF CONTENT

CHAPTER FIVE 65

CHAPTER SIX 8₇

CHAPTER SEVEN..................................101

CHAPTER EIGHT..................................111

CHAPTER TEN 129

CHAPTER ELEVEN 143

CONCLUSION 149

CHAPTER ONE

WELCOME TO TAIPEI CITY

Taipei City is a modern and vibrant metropolis located in the northern part of Taiwan. It is the political, economic, and cultural center of the country, as well as one of the most popular tourist destinations in Asia. The city is home to a diverse population of over 2.6 million people, with Mandarin Chinese being the official language.

Taipei City is known for its modern infrastructure and towering skyscrapers, such as the iconic Taipei 101, which was the tallest building in the world when it was completed in 2004. However, the city also boasts a rich cultural heritage, with temples, museums, and historic landmarks that offer a glimpse into its past.

One of the most famous landmarks in Taipei City is the Chiang Kai-shek Memorial Hall, which was built in honor of the former president of the Republic of China. The hall is located in a park-like setting and features traditional Chinese architecture, as well as a large bronze statue of Chiang Kai-shek.

Another popular attraction in Taipei City is the National Palace Museum, which houses over

700,000 ancient Chinese artifacts and artworks. The museum is home to one of the largest collections of Chinese art in the world, including imperial jade carvings, ceramics, and calligraphy.

Taipei City is also known for its bustling night markets, which offer a wide variety of food, drink, and souvenirs. The most famous night market in the city is the Shilin Night Market, which features hundreds of food stalls selling everything from stinky tofu to grilled squid.

The people of Taipei City are friendly and hospitable, and visitors can expect to be warmly welcomed wherever they go. The city is also home to a vibrant arts and culture scene, with numerous museums, galleries, and performing arts venues.

In recent years, Taipei City has become known for its innovative technology and design industries. The city is home to numerous startups and incubators, as well as some of the world's largest technology companies.

Overall, Taipei City is a must-visit destination for any traveler to Taiwan. With its combination of modern amenities, rich cultural heritage, and friendly people, it offers a unique and unforgettable experience that will stay with visitors for a lifetime.

History Of Taipei City

The history of Taipei City dates back over 300 years. The area where the city now stands was originally inhabited by the Ketagalan, an indigenous tribe of Taiwan. In the early 18th century, Chinese immigrants began to settle in the area, attracted by its fertile land and strategic location near the Tamsui River.

The first settlements in the area were small fishing and farming communities, but the population of the area grew rapidly over the years. In 1875, Taipei City was officially established as a provincial capital during the Qing Dynasty. The city was named Taipei, which means "North of Taipeikang", a reference to a nearby riverbank where clothes were washed.

During the Japanese occupation of Taiwan in the early 20th century, Taipei City underwent significant development and modernization. The Japanese built many of the city's most famous landmarks, including the Taipei Guest House and the Presidential Office Building. They also introduced new technologies, such as electricity and telephones, to the city.

After World War II, Taiwan became a part of the Republic of China, and Taipei City became the capital of the newly formed government. During this time, the city continued to grow and develop, with new infrastructure projects and urbanization initiatives.

In the 1980s and 1990s, Taipei City underwent a period of rapid modernization and economic growth. The city's skyline was transformed by the construction of modern skyscrapers, including the iconic Taipei 101 tower. The city also became a major center for technology and manufacturing, with companies such as Acer and Asus headquartered there.

Today, Taipei City is a thriving metropolis that is known for its rich history, vibrant culture, and modern amenities. Visitors to the city can explore its many museums and historical landmarks, as well as enjoy its bustling night markets and street food scene. The city's history and culture are still visible in its architecture, festivals, and traditions, making it a fascinating destination for any traveler.

Geography And Climate

Geography

Taipei City's geography is fascinating and unique, making it a must-visit destination for tourists. The city is located in a basin surrounded by mountains, which provide a stunning backdrop to the city's skyline and offer plenty of opportunities for outdoor activities such as hiking, mountain biking, and rock climbing.

The mountains surrounding Taipei City are part of the Xueshan Range, which is a subrange of the Central Mountain Range that runs through Taiwan. These mountains offer numerous hiking trails, ranging from easy to challenging, that provide stunning views of the city and surrounding landscapes.

One of the most popular hiking trails in Taipei City is the Elephant Mountain Trail. This trail takes about 20-30 minutes to hike to the top and offers panoramic views of the city's skyline. The Xiangshan Trail is another popular hiking trail that offers stunning views of Taipei 101, the iconic skyscraper that dominates the city's skyline.

In addition to the mountains, the Tamsui River runs through Taipei City, dividing it into northern and southern districts. The river's banks are a popular destination for cycling, jogging, and picnicking, and there are several parks located along the river that offer a peaceful escape from the city's hustle and bustle.

Taipei City's location also makes it an ideal base for exploring other parts of Taiwan. The high-speed rail network connects Taipei City to other cities in Taiwan, such as Taichung and Kaohsiung, making it easy for visitors to explore the island.

Overall, Taipei City's geography provides a stunning backdrop to the city's skyline and offers plenty of opportunities for outdoor activities and exploration. Whether you're looking to hike, cycle, or simply relax by the river, Taipei City's geography has something for everyone.

Climate

Taipei City's climate is classified as a humid subtropical climate. The city has a relatively warm and humid climate all year round, with an average annual temperature of around 23°C (73°F). The summer months, from June to August, are the hottest and most humid, with temperatures averaging around 30°C (86°F) and high humidity levels.

The rainy season in Taipei City is typically from May to September, with occasional typhoons or tropical storms that can cause heavy rainfall and strong winds. Visitors should be aware of the weather forecast and take appropriate precautions during typhoon season, such as carrying an umbrella and staying indoors if necessary.

During the winter months, from December to February, temperatures can drop to around 10°C

(50°F), making it a bit chilly. However, the weather is generally dry and sunny, with occasional rain or snow at higher elevations.

The best time to visit Taipei City is during the spring and fall seasons, from March to May and September to November, respectively. The weather during these seasons is generally cooler and drier, making it more comfortable for outdoor activities such as hiking, cycling, and exploring the city's famous night markets.

Overall, visitors to Taipei City should be prepared for the hot and humid climate, especially during the summer months. Wearing lightweight, breathable clothing and carrying a water bottle is recommended to stay comfortable while exploring the city. Additionally, it's important to stay hydrated and protect yourself from the sun, especially during outdoor activities.

Natural Features

Taipei City's hot springs are a popular attraction for both locals and tourists. There are several hot spring resorts located within an hour's drive of Taipei City, such as Beitou Hot Spring and Wulai Hot Spring. These resorts offer a range of services, including private hot spring baths, spa treatments, and traditional Taiwanese meals.

The city's mountainous terrain also provides several scenic hiking trails. These trails range from easy to challenging and offer visitors a chance to escape the hustle and bustle of the city and enjoy nature. For example, Elephant Mountain Trail is a popular trail that takes about 20-30 minutes to hike to the top, offering panoramic views of Taipei City's skyline.

Infrastructure

Taipei City's transportation system is modern, efficient, and affordable. The Taipei Metro, also known as the MRT, is a subway system that covers most parts of the city. It's easy to use, with signs and announcements in English, and fares are based on the distance traveled.

The city also has an extensive bus network, with buses that run 24 hours a day. Visitors can use their EasyCard, a rechargeable card that can be used on all forms of public transportation, to pay for bus fares.

Taipei City's infrastructure also includes several bike rental services, which are a great way to explore the city's bike-friendly roads and bike paths.

In conclusion, Taipei City's unique geography and climate make it a fascinating destination for tourists. Its natural features, including hot springs and scenic hiking trails, offer visitors a chance to relax and unwind in nature. The city's modern infrastructure, including its public transportation system, makes it easy for visitors to explore and enjoy all that Taipei City has to offer.

Culture And People

Taipei City is a city that is renowned for its warm and hospitable people. The people of Taipei are known for being friendly and welcoming, making it an excellent destination for travelers. The city has a diverse culture that is a result of its unique history and the blend of various cultural influences.

Cultural Diversity

Taipei City is a city that is steeped in cultural diversity, with a rich history and a blend of different cultural influences. The city has a unique identity that is shaped by its past and the cultures of its people. In this section, we will delve deeper into the cultural diversity of Taipei City.

Chinese Influence

Chinese culture has played a significant role in the development of Taipei City. The city's architecture, language, and customs have been shaped by Chinese traditions. For example, the city's historic architecture reflects the styles of different Chinese dynasties, such as the Qing and Ming dynasties.

Taipei's people have also preserved Chinese customs, such as the practice of ancestor worship.

Japanese Influence

Japan occupied Taiwan from 1895 to 1945, and during this time, Japanese culture had a significant impact on Taipei City. The city's streets and buildings were redesigned to reflect Japanese architecture, and the Japanese language was widely spoken. Many of Taipei's famous landmarks, such as the Taipei 101 skyscraper, were built during the Japanese occupation.

Indigenous Taiwanese Culture

Indigenous Taiwanese culture is an essential part of Taipei City's cultural diversity. The city is home to several indigenous tribes, such as the Atayal and the Paiwan. Visitors can learn about these cultures by visiting the National Museum of Prehistory and the Taipei Indigenous Peoples Cultural Park. Taipei's people have also preserved the traditions of these tribes, such as their unique music, dance, and crafts.

Western Influence

Western influence has also shaped Taipei City's cultural diversity. The city's colonial past has left a lasting impact on its architecture, language, and customs. For example, the city's neoclassical buildings reflect Western architectural styles. Taipei's people have also adopted Western customs, such as celebrating Christmas and Valentine's Day.

Taipei City's cultural diversity is a result of its unique history and the blend of different cultural influences. Visitors can experience the city's Chinese, Japanese, indigenous Taiwanese, and Western cultures through its architecture, language, cuisine, and customs. The city's people have preserved these traditions, making Taipei City a fascinating destination for travelers who want to experience a rich and diverse cultural heritage.

Religion

Taipei City is a city that is rich in religious diversity. Its people practice a range of religions, including Buddhism, Taoism, Christianity, and Islam. Religion is an essential part of Taipei's culture, and visitors can witness the city's religious traditions by visiting its temples, churches, and mosques.

Buddhism

Buddhism is the most widely practiced religion in Taipei City. Visitors can witness its influence by visiting temples such as the Longshan Temple, which is one of the oldest and most famous Buddhist temples in Taipei City. It was built in 1738 and has been destroyed and rebuilt multiple times. The temple's architecture is a blend of Chinese and Taiwanese styles, and it features various halls and shrines dedicated to different Buddhist deities.

Taoism

Taoism is another popular religion in Taipei City. Visitors can witness its influence by visiting temples such as the Xingtian Temple, which is dedicated to the god Guan Yu, who is worshipped as a symbol of loyalty and righteousness. The temple features ornate decorations, including dragon sculptures and intricate carvings.

Christianity

Christianity is a minority religion in Taipei City, but it has a significant presence. Visitors can attend mass or services at various churches, including St. Christopher's Church, which is a Roman Catholic church that was built in the 1930s. The church features beautiful stained glass windows and a beautiful organ.

Islam

Islam is a minority religion in Taipei City, but it has a growing presence. The Taipei Grand Mosque is the city's largest mosque and is a must-visit for visitors who want to experience Islamic culture. The mosque features traditional Islamic architecture and has facilities for prayers and other religious activities.

Religious Festivals

Religious festivals are an essential part of Taipei's culture, and they provide visitors with a unique opportunity to witness the city's religious traditions.

For example, the Lunar New Year is one of the most significant festivals in Taipei City, and it is celebrated with dragon and lion dances, fireworks, and traditional food. The Ghost Festival is another important religious festival that is held in Taipei City, and it is a time when people pay their respects to their ancestors.

Taipei City's religious diversity is an essential aspect of its culture. Visitors can witness the city's religious traditions by visiting its temples, churches, and mosques, attending religious services, or experiencing its religious festivals. Religion is an integral part of Taipei's culture, and it provides visitors with a unique opportunity to experience the city's traditions and customs.

Language

Taipei City is a vibrant and bustling city, where Mandarin Chinese is the official language. However, English is also widely spoken, especially in tourist areas. Visitors can also hear other languages spoken, such as Hokkien, Cantonese, and Taiwanese.

Mandarin Chinese

Mandarin Chinese is the most widely spoken language in Taipei City. It is the official language of Taiwan, and it is spoken by over 70% of the population. Mandarin Chinese is also the standard language of business and education in the country.

English
English is widely spoken in Taipei City, especially in tourist areas. Most people in the service industry, such as hotel staff and tour guides, are fluent in English. Visitors will have no trouble communicating with locals, and they can easily navigate the city using English signage and maps.

Taiwanese
Taiwanese, also known as Hokkien, is another language that is spoken in Taipei City. It is a dialect of Minnan, a Chinese language family that originated from Fujian province in mainland China. Taiwanese is mostly spoken by the older generation, but it is still used in daily conversation and can be heard in traditional markets and local neighborhoods.

Cantonese
Cantonese is another dialect of Chinese that is spoken in Taipei City. It is mostly spoken by immigrants from Hong Kong and Guangdong province in mainland China. Visitors may hear Cantonese spoken in restaurants and hotels that cater to the Hong Kong and Guangdong market.

Other Languages

Apart from Mandarin Chinese, English, Taiwanese, and Cantonese, Taipei City is home to various immigrant communities, which have brought their own languages and cultures to the city. For instance, there are significant Japanese and Filipino communities in Taipei City, and their respective languages can be heard in their communities and establishments.

Taipei City's linguistic diversity is a reflection of its cultural richness and history. Visitors can experience a variety of languages and dialects, making it an exciting and unique destination. With Mandarin Chinese and English being widely spoken, communication is not a barrier, making it easy for visitors to navigate the city.

Cuisine

Taipei City is a paradise for food lovers, with a diverse range of cuisine that reflects its history and cultural influences. Taiwanese cuisine is a fusion of different culinary traditions, including Chinese, Japanese, and indigenous Taiwanese cuisines. In this chapter, we'll explore some of the must-try dishes and dining options that Taipei City has to offer.

Must-Try Dishes In Taipei

Beef Noodle Soup: This is a classic Taiwanese dish that is a must-try for any visitor. It's a hearty soup made with slow-cooked beef, noodles, and various spices and seasonings.

Xiaolongbao: These are steamed buns filled with meat, seafood, or vegetables. They are a staple food in Taipei's night markets and are best enjoyed hot and fresh.

Oyster Omelette: This is a popular Taiwanese street food that consists of a savory omelette filled with oysters and vegetables. It's often topped with a sweet and spicy sauce.

Bubble Tea: This Taiwanese drink has taken the world by storm. It's a sweet and refreshing drink made with tea, milk, and tapioca pearls. Bubble tea shops can be found throughout the city, and visitors can choose from a variety of flavors and toppings.

Dining Options

Night Markets: Taipei City is famous for its night markets, which offer a vast array of street food and local delicacies. Some of the most popular night markets include Shilin Night Market and Raohe Street Night Market.

Michelin-Starred Restaurants: Taipei City is home to several Michelin-starred restaurants that offer world-class dining experiences. These include RAW, MUME, and The Guest House.

Taiwanese-Style Hot Pot: Hot pot is a popular dining option in Taipei City, and there are many restaurants that specialize in Taiwanese-style hot pot. The hot pot consists of a simmering pot of broth and a variety of meats, seafood, and vegetables that are cooked at the table.

Modern Taiwanese Cuisine: Taipei City is also home to many restaurants that serve modern Taiwanese cuisine. These restaurants combine traditional Taiwanese flavors and cooking techniques with modern culinary techniques.

In summary, Taipei City's diverse cuisine is one of its biggest attractions. Visitors can enjoy a wide range of dishes, from classic Taiwanese street food to world-class fine dining. Taipei City's food scene reflects its history and cultural influences, and visitors can experience the city's unique culinary culture by exploring its night markets, trying its must-try dishes, and dining at its Michelin-starred restaurants.

Arts And Culture

Taipei City has a vibrant arts and culture scene that offers a wide range of experiences for visitors. From traditional art forms to contemporary exhibitions, the city has something to offer for everyone. In this section, we will explore Taipei's arts and culture scene in more detail.

Performing Arts
Taipei City is home to numerous performing arts venues that showcase traditional and contemporary art forms. The National Theater and Concert Hall is the city's premier performing arts venue, featuring performances of traditional Chinese opera, music, and dance. The venue also hosts international performances from around the world, making it a must-visit destination for performing arts enthusiasts.

Traditional Arts
Taipei City has a rich tradition of folk art, music, and crafts. The National Center for Traditional Arts is a cultural park that offers visitors a chance to experience traditional Taiwanese art forms. The center features exhibitions on paper cutting, woodcarving, and other crafts, as well as performances of traditional music and dance.

Contemporary Art
Taipei City is also known for its contemporary art scene. The Taipei Fine Arts Museum is a leading contemporary art museum in Asia, showcasing works from local and international artists. The museum hosts exhibitions on various art forms, including painting, sculpture, and multimedia installations. The museum's rooftop garden offers a

stunning view of the city skyline, making it a popular spot for photography enthusiasts.

Literature
Taipei City is also home to numerous literary works that reflect the city's cultural heritage. Visitors can explore the works of prominent Taiwanese authors at the Taipei City Library. The library houses over 800,000 books, including rare manuscripts and first editions of classic works.

Cuisine and Culture:
Taipei City's culinary scene is an essential aspect of its culture. Food plays a significant role in Taiwanese culture, and Taipei's night markets and street food stalls offer visitors a chance to taste traditional Taiwanese cuisine. Visitors can learn about the history and preparation of Taiwanese dishes by taking cooking classes or joining food tours.

Taipei City's arts and culture scene is a reflection of the city's rich history and diverse cultural influences. From traditional arts to contemporary exhibitions, the city offers visitors a chance to explore a wide range of cultural experiences. Taipei's culinary scene is also an essential aspect of its culture, offering visitors a chance to taste traditional Taiwanese cuisine.

In conclusion, Taipei City is a fascinating destination that offers something for everyone. Its rich history, stunning natural scenery, and vibrant culture make it a must-visit destination for any traveler. In the following chapters, we'll explore the best attractions, food, and experiences that Taipei City has to offer.

Currency And Exchange

The official currency of Taipei City is the New Taiwan Dollar (TWD), which is commonly referred to as simply "dollar" in Taiwan. The New Taiwan Dollar is issued by the Central Bank of the Republic of China and is available in banknotes and coins.

Banknotes in circulation in Taipei City come in denominations of NT$100, NT$500, NT$1000, and NT$2000. Coins come in denominations of NT$1, NT$5, NT$10, NT$20, and NT$50. While the New Taiwan Dollar is the official currency, some establishments in Taipei City also accept US dollars, especially in the more touristy areas.

If you need to exchange currency, there are several options available in Taipei City. Banks and currency exchange offices are widely available, especially in the tourist areas, and offer competitive rates. You can also exchange currency at the airport, but rates may be slightly higher than other exchange offices in the city.

Most major credit cards are accepted in Taipei City, including Visa, Mastercard, and American Express. However, it is always a good idea to have some cash on hand, especially if you plan on visiting smaller shops, markets, or street vendors.

It is also worth noting that Taiwan has a relatively low cost of living, so you may find that your money goes further in Taipei City than in other major cities around the world. Overall, Taipei City is a friendly and convenient destination for travelers, and exchanging currency is a straightforward process.

CHAPTER TWO

ESSENTIAL THINGS TO PACK ON YOUR TRIP TO TAIPEI

Taipei, the bustling capital city of Taiwan, is a popular destination for tourists from around the world. Whether you're visiting for the first time or returning for another adventure, packing the right items can make all the difference in ensuring a comfortable and enjoyable trip.

Here are some of the essential things to pack for your Taipei trip:

Travel documents

Make sure to have a valid passport or ID card, as well as any necessary visas for your trip. It's also a good idea to have a printed or electronic copy of your flight itinerary and travel insurance documents. Keep all of these documents in a secure place while you travel.

Money and payment methods

It's a good idea to bring some cash in the local currency, TWD, for small purchases or in case you have trouble with your credit or debit card. Many places in Taipei accept credit cards, but it's still a good idea to have some cash on hand. Make sure to inform your bank of your travel plans so they don't flag your card for fraud. Traveler's checks can be useful if you prefer not to carry cash, but they may not be accepted everywhere.

Electronics and chargers

Smartphones and cameras are useful for capturing memories and navigating the city. Make sure to bring a charger for each device, and consider bringing a power bank if you plan to be out for long periods of time. Taipei uses a 110-volt power supply, so if your electronics use a different plug type, be sure to bring a universal power adapter.

Clothing and footwear

Taipei can be hot and humid, especially in the summer months, so lightweight and breathable clothing is recommended. Comfortable walking shoes are a must, as Taipei is a city best explored on foot. Sandals or flip-flops are also useful for trips to the beach or hot springs. Be sure to check the weather forecast before your trip and pack accordingly.

Personal care items

Sunscreen and insect repellent are important for protecting your skin from the sun and bugs. Bring personal hygiene items like toothbrushes and toothpaste, as well as any prescription medications you need. Make sure to pack enough medication for your entire trip, and consider bringing a copy of your prescription in case you need to refill it while you're in Taipei.

Travel accessories

A daypack or backpack is useful for carrying essentials like a water bottle, sunscreen, and snacks. A travel pillow and blanket can be helpful for longer flights, and a guidebook or map of Taipei can help you navigate the city. Taipei's tap water is safe to drink, so consider bringing a refillable water bottle to save money and reduce waste.

Optional items

A travel lock can provide added security for your luggage or hotel room. A portable Wi-Fi device can be useful if you need constant internet access while you're out and about. Language translation apps like Google Translate can be helpful if you don't speak

Mandarin, but many people in Taipei speak at least some English.

Remember to pack light and avoid bringing anything you don't really need. You can always buy items you forget or need in Taipei, and there are plenty of shopping options available. By packing smart and being prepared, you can have a comfortable and enjoyable trip to Taipei!

Entry Requirements And Visa Regulations

Entry Requirements

Taipei is a welcoming city for travelers from all over the world. Visitors to Taipei are required to present a valid passport with at least six months of remaining validity upon arrival. Some nationalities are also required to apply for a visa before traveling to Taiwan.

Visa Regulations

Visa-exempt countries:

Citizens of certain countries are eligible for visa-exempt entry into Taiwan. Citizens of these countries can stay in Taiwan for up to 90 days without a visa. Here is a list of some of the visa free countries

- New Zealand
- Norway
- Poland
- Portugal
- Spain
- Sweden
- Switzerland
- U.K.
- U.S.A.
- Australia
- Austria
- Belgium
- Finland
- France e.t.c

Visa-exempt countries for a shorter duration:

Citizens of some countries can stay in Taiwan visa-free for a shorter duration:

Brunei and Thailand: up to 14 days
Philippines: up to 14 days (if holding a valid visa or permanent residency from Australia, Canada, Japan, New Zealand, Schengen countries, U.K., or U.S.A., the length of stay can be extended up to 59 days)

Cambodia, India, Indonesia, Laos, Malaysia, Myanmar, and Vietnam: up to 30 days

Visa on Arrival
Citizens of certain countries can apply for a visa on arrival for a fee upon their arrival in Taiwan. The visa on arrival is valid for up to 30 days:

Bahrain, Kuwait, Oman, Saudi Arabia, and the United Arab Emirates.

Visa Required
Citizens of other countries that are not listed are required to apply for a visa before traveling to Taiwan. The visa application process usually takes 3 to 5 working days.

Applying for a visa
Visa applications can be made through Taiwanese embassies or consulates in your home country. The application process usually includes submitting the required documents, such as a passport, a completed visa application form, and other supporting documents.

In summary, travelers from many countries are eligible for visa-exempt entry into Taiwan, while citizens of some countries can apply for a visa on arrival. Citizens of other countries are required to apply for a visa before traveling to Taiwan. It is important to check the current visa requirements and regulations before making travel arrangements to Taipei.

Best Time To Travel To Taipei

Taipei is a vibrant city in Taiwan that attracts tourists from all over the world. Its mix of traditional and modern culture, delicious cuisine, and stunning natural beauty makes it a popular destination year-round. However, the best time to visit Taipei depends on your personal preferences and what you want to experience during your trip.

Spring (March - May)
Spring is one of the best times to visit Taipei, as the weather is mild, and the city is alive with blooming flowers and cherry blossoms. The average temperature in Taipei during spring is around 20-25°C (68-77°F), making it a comfortable season to explore the city's parks, gardens, and outdoor attractions. This is also the season for many cultural events, such as the Taipei Lantern Festival and the Qingming Festival.

Summer (June - August)
Summer in Taipei can be hot and humid, with temperatures averaging around 28-33°C (82-91°F). Despite the weather, summer is still a popular time to visit Taipei, especially for outdoor activities such as hiking in the nearby mountains or visiting the

beaches in the surrounding area. However, it is important to be prepared for the heat and humidity, especially if you are not used to it.

Fall (September - November)
Fall is another excellent time to visit Taipei, as the weather cools down, and the city is draped in beautiful fall foliage. Temperatures in Taipei during fall range from 20-28°C (68-82°F), making it a comfortable season for outdoor activities such as hiking, cycling, and visiting the night markets. This is also the season for many cultural events, such as the Mid-Autumn Festival and the Taipei International Flora Expo.

Winter (December - February)
Winter is the coolest season in Taipei, with temperatures ranging from 13-20°C (55-68°F). While it may be too cold for some outdoor activities, winter is still a great time to visit Taipei, especially if you enjoy winter sports such as skiing and snowboarding. It is also the season for many festivals and events, such as the New Year's Eve fireworks display at Taipei 101 and the Pingxi Sky Lantern Festival.

Overall, the best time to visit Taipei depends on what you want to experience during your trip. If you are looking for mild weather and blooming flowers, spring is the best time to go. If you want to enjoy outdoor activities and summer festivals, then summer is the season for you. If you enjoy the fall foliage and cultural events, then fall is the best season to visit. Finally, if you like winter sports and festivals, then winter is the perfect time to explore Taipei.

CHAPTER THREE

GETTING TO TAIPEI CITY

Taipei City is a bustling metropolis located in the north of Taiwan. The city is well connected to other parts of the country and the world, making it easy for tourists and travelers to visit. Here are some popular transportation options for getting to Taipei City:

By Air

Taipei City has two airports that serve the city, Taiwan Taoyuan International Airport (TPE) and Taipei Songshan Airport (TSA).

Taiwan Taoyuan International Airport (TPE) is the main airport serving Taipei City, and it's the largest airport in Taiwan. It is located about 40 kilometers west of Taipei City, and it serves as a hub for many international airlines. Some of the major airlines that operate at TPE include EVA Air, China Airlines, Cathay Pacific, and Japan Airlines.

Getting to Taipei City from TPE is easy, with several transportation options available:

Taxi

Taxis are readily available at TPE, and they are a convenient option for travelers who want to get to their destination quickly. However, they are also the most expensive option. Taxis charge a flat rate of NT$1,200 (approximately $42 USD) for a one-way trip to Taipei City. The trip takes approximately 40 minutes, depending on traffic.

Airport Shuttle Bus
The airport shuttle bus is a more affordable option than a taxi. The bus stops at several locations in Taipei City, including Taipei Main Station, Ximen, and Zhongxiao Dunhua. The fare for the shuttle bus ranges from NT$125 to NT$310 (approximately $4 to $11 USD) depending on your destination. The trip takes approximately 60 minutes, depending on traffic.

Metro
The Taipei Metro, also known as the MRT, is a convenient and affordable option for getting to Taipei City from TPE. The airport MRT station is located in Terminal 1, and it connects to the Taoyuan Airport MRT line. The fare for the MRT ranges from depending on your destination. The trip takes approximately 35 minutes to get to Taipei Main Station.

Taipei Songshan Airport (TSA) is located in the city center, and it mainly serves domestic flights and international flights to and from some Asian cities. Some of the airlines that operate at TSA include China Airlines, EVA Air, and Uni Air.

Getting to Taipei City from TSA is easy, with several transportation options available:

Metro
The airport MRT line also stops at Taipei Songshan Airport, and it connects to the Taoyuan Airport MRT line. The fare for the MRT ranges depending on your destination. The trip takes approximately 20 minutes to get to Taipei Main Station.

Taxi
Taxis are readily available at TSA, and they are a convenient option for travelers who want to get to their destination quickly. Taxis charge a metered rate based on distance traveled. The trip takes approximately 15-20 minutes, depending on traffic.

In summary, Taipei City is well-served by two airports, Taiwan Taoyuan International Airport (TPE) and Taipei Songshan Airport (TSA). Both airports offer several transportation options, including taxis, airport shuttle buses, and the Taipei Metro. No matter which airport you arrive at, getting to Taipei City is easy and convenient, making it an ideal destination for travelers and tourists alike.

By Train

Taipei City has two major train stations, Taipei Main Station and Songshan Station. These stations offer both the Taiwan High Speed Rail (THSR) and the Taiwan Railways Administration (TRA) services, connecting Taipei with other major cities in Taiwan.

Taiwan High-Speed Rail (THSR):
The Taiwan High-Speed Rail (THSR) is a high-speed train service that runs along the west coast of Taiwan, connecting Taipei City to major cities such as Taoyuan, Taichung, Tainan, and Kaohsiung. The THSR trains are fast, efficient, and comfortable, making them a popular choice for travelers who want to quickly and conveniently travel between major cities in Taiwan.

To take the THSR to Taipei City, you can board the train at either Taipei Station or Nangang Station, which are both located in the city. The THSR station in Taipei City is connected to the metro system, so it's easy to transfer to other parts of the city.

Taiwan Railways Administration (TRA):
The Taiwan Railways Administration (TRA) is a nationwide railway network that connects all major cities and towns in Taiwan. TRA trains are divided into four types: express, local, stopping, and commuter, each with different stops and fares.

To take the TRA to Taipei City, you can board the train at either Taipei Main Station or Songshan Station, both of which are located in the city. Taipei Main Station is the main transportation hub in Taipei and it serves both the THSR and the TRA. Songshan Station mainly serves TRA trains that run along the east coast of Taiwan.

It's important to note that the TRA trains are more affordable than the THSR, but they take longer to reach their destinations. However, the TRA trains offer a scenic route, passing through the beautiful countryside and mountains of Taiwan, so they can be a great option for those who want to enjoy the scenery.

Overall, traveling to Taipei City by train is a convenient and affordable option, especially for those who want to explore other parts of Taiwan as well. Both the THSR and TRA offer fast and efficient service, with Taipei City being well connected to major cities and towns across Taiwan.

By Bus

Taipei City is well connected to other parts of Taiwan by intercity buses. There are several bus stations in Taipei that serve as transportation hubs for intercity buses. Some of the popular bus stations in Taipei include Taipei Bus Station, Taipei City Hall Bus Station, and Taipei Songshan Bus Station.

Taipei Bus Station, located in the Zhongzheng District of Taipei, is the largest bus station in Taiwan and serves as the main hub for intercity bus transportation in Taipei. It is located near Taipei Main Station and is easily accessible by metro. The bus station has several floors with different bus companies operating on each floor. There are a wide variety of bus companies that operate from Taipei Bus Station, offering services to various parts of Taiwan.

Taipei City Hall Bus Station is another popular bus station in Taipei that is located in the Xinyi District. It mainly serves buses traveling to and from the eastern part of Taiwan. It is easily accessible by metro, and there are several bus companies that operate from this bus station.

Taipei Songshan Bus Station is located near Taipei Songshan Airport and mainly serves buses traveling to and from the northern part of Taiwan. It is easily accessible by metro and there are several bus companies that operate from this bus station.

There are also express buses that connect Taipei to other major cities in Taiwan, such as Kaohsiung and Taichung. These express buses are usually more expensive than regular intercity buses, but they offer a more comfortable and faster way to travel between cities.

When traveling by bus in Taipei, it's important to note that seats on buses can fill up quickly, especially during peak travel times. It's recommended to purchase bus tickets in advance to ensure a seat on the bus. Additionally, some bus companies offer online ticket booking services, which can be more convenient and save time.

In summary, traveling to Taipei City by intercity bus is a popular and affordable option. Taipei has several bus stations that serve as transportation hubs for intercity buses, with Taipei Bus Station being the largest and most popular. Express buses are also available for travel to other major cities in Taiwan. When traveling by bus in Taipei, it's recommended to purchase tickets in advance to ensure a seat on the bus.

By Car

If you prefer the flexibility and independence of traveling by car, it's possible to drive to Taipei City. Taiwan's National Highway No. 1 runs north-south through the island and passes through Taipei City. Additionally, there are several other national and provincial highways that connect Taipei to other parts of Taiwan.

However, it's important to note that driving in Taipei City can be challenging due to heavy traffic and limited parking. Taipei is a densely populated city with narrow roads and a high volume of cars, scooters, and pedestrians. Traffic congestion is common, especially during rush hours and on weekends. Additionally, parking can be difficult to find, and street parking is often limited and subject to strict parking regulations.

If you plan on driving in Taipei City, it's recommended that you rent a car with a GPS system or a navigation app on your smartphone. This will help you navigate the city's complex road network and find the best routes to your destination. Most car rental companies in Taipei require a valid international driver's license, a credit card, and a minimum age requirement of 21 or 25 years old.

It's also important to be aware of Taiwan's traffic rules and regulations, which are similar to those in other countries. Drivers must drive on the right side of the road and obey speed limits, traffic signals, and signs. Seat belts are mandatory for all passengers, and driving under the influence of alcohol or drugs is strictly prohibited.

When driving in Taipei City, it's important to be patient and cautious, especially when sharing the road with scooters and pedestrians. It's also recommended that you avoid driving during rush hours and on weekends if possible, as traffic congestion can be particularly severe during these times.

Traveling to Taipei City by car is possible, but it's important to be aware of the challenges and potential difficulties associated with driving in a busy and crowded city. If you decide to drive in Taipei, be sure to plan ahead, follow traffic rules and regulations, and be patient and cautious on the road.

Once you arrive in Taipei City, you can easily get around the city using public transportation, such as the metro, buses, and taxis. It's important to note that the Taipei Metro is a convenient and affordable way to travel around the city, as it covers most of the popular tourist destinations and it's easy to navigate. Additionally, there are several car rental companies in Taipei if you prefer to explore the city on your own.

In summary, Taipei City is well connected to other parts of Taiwan and the world, with several transportation options available, including air, train, bus, and car. With so many transportation options available, getting to Taipei City is easy and convenient, making it an ideal destination for travelers and tourists alike.

CHAPTER FOUR

ACCOMMODATION IN TAIPEI CITY

Taipei City offers a wide range of accommodation options to suit all budgets and preferences. It doesn't matter if you're looking for a luxurious hotel, a budget-friendly hostel, or something in between, Taipei has something for everyone.

Types Of Accommodation

Taipei City offers a wide range of accommodation options to suit all budgets and preferences. Whether you're looking for a luxurious hotel, a budget-friendly hostel, or something in between, Taipei has something for everyone.

Hotels

Taipei City offers a wide range of hotels, from budget options to luxurious five-star properties. Many of the top hotels are located in the city center, particularly in the Xinyi District, which is the city's financial and commercial hub. Here are some of the types of hotels you'll find in Taipei:'

Budget Hotels

Budget hotels in Taipei City are a good option for travelers who want to save money on accommodation. These hotels typically offer basic amenities such as free Wi-Fi, air conditioning, and a private bathroom. They may also offer breakfast, but it's often simple and not included in the room rate. These hotels are usually located in the outer districts of the city, but some are still conveniently located near public transportation.

Here are some of the most popular budget hotels in Taipei City:

CityInn Hotel: CityInn Hotel has several locations throughout Taipei City, including in the Zhongshan and Ximending districts. These hotels offer modern and clean rooms at an affordable price.

iTaipei Service Apartments: iTaipei Service Apartments is located in the Da'an District and offers spacious rooms with kitchenettes at a budget-friendly price.

Cai She Hotel: Cai She Hotel is located in the Xinyi District and offers cozy and clean rooms at an affordable price.

Mid-Range Hotels

Mid-range hotels in Taipei City offer more amenities than budget hotels. These hotels usually offer a fitness center, a restaurant, and a conference room. They may also have a more central location in the city, such as in the Xinyi District. Mid-range hotels are a good option for travelers who want a bit more comfort and convenience without breaking the bank. Here are some of the most popular mid-range hotels in Taipei City:

Green World Hotels: Green World Hotels has several locations throughout Taipei City, including in the Ximending and Songshan districts. These hotels offer comfortable and modern rooms at a mid-range price.

Just Sleep Hotel: Just Sleep Hotel has several locations throughout Taipei City, including in the Zhongzheng and Ximending districts. These hotels offer clean and comfortable rooms at a mid-range price.

Taipei Fullerton Hotel: Taipei Fullerton Hotel is located in the Da'an District and offers spacious and comfortable rooms with a mid-range price.

Luxury Hotels

Luxury hotels in Taipei City offer world-class amenities and service. These hotels usually have a central location in the city, such as in the Xinyi

District. They offer amenities such as a spa, a fitness center, a swimming pool, and several restaurants. Luxury hotels are a good option for travelers who want to indulge in a bit of luxury during their stay in Taipei City. Here are some of the most popular luxury hotels in Taipei City:

Mandarin Oriental Taipei: Mandarin Oriental Taipei is located in the Da'an District and offers luxurious rooms and suites, several restaurants, a spa, and a fitness center.

W Taipei: W Taipei is located in the Xinyi District and offers modern and luxurious rooms and suites, a rooftop bar, a spa, and a fitness center.

Grand Hyatt Taipei: Grand Hyatt Taipei is located in the Xinyi District and offers luxurious rooms and suites, several restaurants, a spa, a fitness center, and a swimming pool.

Hostels

Hostels are a popular option for budget travelers and backpackers. They offer shared and private rooms at affordable prices, and many provide a friendly and social atmosphere. In Taipei City, there are a variety of hostels to choose from, ranging from basic and no-frills to more upscale and luxurious.

One of the benefits of staying in a hostel is the opportunity to meet other travelers from around the world. Many hostels organize social events and activities, making it easy to meet other people and explore the city together. Some hostels also offer shared spaces such as common rooms or kitchens, which provide a comfortable place to relax and socialize with other guests.

When choosing a hostel in Taipei City, there are a few things to consider. Location is important, and it's a good idea to choose a hostel that's close to public transportation or within walking distance of major attractions. Safety is also a priority, so it's important to choose a hostel with secure locks and a safe place to store your belongings.

Here are some of the top hostels in Taipei City:

Taipei Hostel: This hostel is located in the Da'an District, a trendy area known for its shopping and dining. It offers clean and comfortable dorms and private rooms, with amenities such as air conditioning, free Wi-Fi, and a shared kitchen and lounge.

Homey Hostel: This hostel is also located in the Da'an District, and offers a friendly and social atmosphere. It has private and shared rooms available, as well as a rooftop terrace and common areas for guests to relax and socialize.

Flip Flop Hostel: This hostel is located in the Ximending District, a vibrant area known for its nightlife and shopping. It offers clean and comfortable rooms at an affordable price, with amenities such as free Wi-Fi, a shared kitchen and lounge, and a rooftop terrace.

Meander Hostel: This hostel is located in the Zhongzheng District, close to major attractions such as the Chiang Kai-shek Memorial Hall and the National Taiwan Museum. It offers private and shared rooms, as well as a common area with a pool table and board games.

Backpackers Inn Taipei: This hostel is located in the Wanhua District, near the famous Longshan Temple. It offers clean and comfortable rooms at an affordable price, with amenities such as free Wi-Fi and a shared kitchen and lounge.

Overall, hostels can be a great option for budget travelers looking for affordable and social accommodation in Taipei City. With so many options to choose from, it's easy to find a hostel that meets your needs and preferences.

Airbnb

Airbnb is a popular option for travelers looking for unique and affordable accommodation options in

Taipei City. As the city continues to grow in popularity as a tourist destination, more and more hosts are listing their properties on Airbnb, offering a diverse range of options for travelers.

Private rooms are a common type of Airbnb listing in Taipei City. These listings offer a private room within a larger apartment or house, where the host may or may not be present during your stay. This is a great option if you want to stay with a local and get insider tips on what to see and do in Taipei. Many hosts are happy to provide recommendations for local restaurants, shops, and attractions.

Entire apartments or houses are also available on Airbnb in Taipei City. These listings offer a private apartment or house for your stay in Taipei, giving you more privacy and independence during your stay. These listings are a good option if you're traveling with a group or family, or if you simply prefer more space and privacy.

In addition to private rooms and entire apartments, Taipei City also has a number of unique Airbnb listings. For example, you can find traditional Taiwanese houses in neighborhoods like Dadaocheng, where you can experience the city's rich cultural heritage. There are also lofts in converted warehouses, giving you a taste of Taipei's hip and creative side.

When booking an Airbnb in Taipei City, it's important to check the location of the listing. Many of the top Airbnb listings are located in popular neighborhoods like Ximending, Da'an, and the Xinyi District, which offer a range of shops, restaurants, and attractions. However, if you're looking for a quieter stay, you may want to consider a listing in one of the city's more residential neighborhoods.

It's also important to read reviews from previous guests before booking an Airbnb in Taipei City. This will give you a sense of the host's hospitality and the quality of the accommodation. Additionally, be sure to communicate with the host before booking to ensure that the listing meets your needs and expectations.

Overall, Airbnb can be a great option for travelers looking for a unique and authentic stay in Taipei City. With a range of options to choose from, you're sure to find a listing that fits your budget and travel style.

Guesthouses

Guesthouses are a popular option for travelers who are looking for a more homely and personal experience. Guesthouses in Taipei are usually smaller than hotels and offer private rooms with shared facilities such as bathrooms, kitchens, and common areas. Here are some of the advantages of staying in a guesthouse in Taipei:

Personalized service: Guesthouse owners and staff are usually more hands-on and able to provide personalized service to their guests. They can give recommendations on local attractions and activities, and can provide tips on how to get around the city.

Local experience: Guesthouses are often located in residential neighborhoods, which provides guests with an opportunity to experience local life and culture in Taipei. Guests can interact with locals and get a feel for the local way of life.

Affordable: Guesthouses are typically more affordable than hotels, making them a good option for budget travelers. They offer basic amenities at a lower cost, and some guesthouses even offer free breakfast.

Social atmosphere: Many guesthouses offer communal areas such as living rooms and kitchens where guests can socialize with each other. This is a great way to meet other travelers and make new friends during your stay in Taipei.

Here are some of the top guesthouses in Taipei:

Dadaocheng Guesthouse: This guesthouse is located in the historic Dadaocheng area and offers private rooms with shared facilities. The guesthouse is housed in a traditional Taiwanese building and has a homely and rustic feel. The staff are friendly and knowledgeable about the local area, and the guesthouse is within walking distance of many local attractions.

Banana Hostel: This guesthouse is located in the trendy Ximending District and offers clean and comfortable rooms at an affordable price. The guesthouse has a friendly and social atmosphere, with a common area where guests can socialize and relax. The staff are helpful and can provide recommendations on local attractions and restaurants.

Taipei Discover Hostel: This guesthouse is located in the bustling Da'an District and offers private rooms with shared facilities. The guesthouse is modern and clean, with a bright and airy common area. The staff are friendly and can provide tips on how to get around the city and what to see and do in Taipei. The guesthouse is within walking distance of many local restaurants and shops.

When choosing a guesthouse in Taipei, it's important to consider the location, the amenities offered, and the price. Some guesthouses may offer more basic facilities, while others may have more luxurious options such as private bathrooms and air conditioning. It's also important to read reviews from previous guests to get an idea of the quality of service and facilities offered.

Overall, guesthouses are a great option for travelers who are looking for a more personal and affordable experience in Taipei. With a range of options available, from rustic and homely to modern and chic, there's sure to be a guesthouse in Taipei that fits your needs and budget.

Serviced Apartment

Serviced apartments are a great option for travelers who are planning an extended stay in Taipei City. These apartments offer the comforts of home, with the added amenities and services of a hotel. Serviced apartments are typically fully furnished and come equipped with a range of amenities such as a fully equipped kitchen, laundry facilities, and daily housekeeping.

Here are some of the top serviced apartments in Taipei City:

Pacific Business Center: This serviced apartment is located in the Xinyi District, which is the financial and commercial hub of Taipei City. The Pacific Business Center offers spacious apartments with modern amenities, including a fully equipped kitchen, free Wi-Fi, and a fitness center. The apartments are also located near many of Taipei's top attractions, including the Taipei 101 Tower, the Taipei World Trade Center, and the Taipei International Convention Center.

Gloria Residence: This serviced apartment is located in the Da'an District, which is a popular neighborhood for expats and business travelers. The Gloria Residence offers luxurious apartments with a range of amenities, including a fully equipped kitchen, a fitness center, and a rooftop garden. The apartments are also located near many of Taipei's top restaurants, cafes, and shops.

L'Arc Hotel: This serviced apartment is located in the Zhongshan District, which is known for its shopping and entertainment options. The L'Arc Hotel offers spacious apartments with a range of amenities, including a fully equipped kitchen, free Wi-Fi, and a fitness center. The apartments are also located near many of Taipei's top shopping destinations, including the Taipei 101 Mall and the Shin Kong Mitsukoshi Department Store.

The Tango Hotel Taipei Nanshi: This serviced apartment is located in the Zhongzheng District, which is home to many of Taipei's cultural and historical landmarks. The Tango Hotel Taipei Nanshi offers luxurious apartments with a range of amenities, including a fully equipped kitchen, a fitness center, and a rooftop garden. The apartments are also located near many of Taipei's top attractions, including the National Taiwan Museum, the Chiang Kai-shek Memorial Hall, and the Presidential Office Building.

Green World Hotels ZhongXiao: This serviced apartment is located in the Da'an District, which is a popular neighborhood for foodies and nightlife. The Green World Hotels ZhongXiao offers spacious apartments with a range of amenities, including a fully equipped kitchen, a fitness center, and a rooftop garden. The apartments are also located near many of Taipei's top restaurants, cafes, and bars.

Overall, serviced apartments in Taipei City offer a comfortable and convenient option for travelers who are planning an extended stay. With their range of amenities and central locations, serviced apartments can provide a home away from home while exploring all that Taipei City has to offer.

Popular Areas To Stay In Taipei City

Taipei City is a bustling metropolis with a wide range of neighborhoods and districts to explore. When it comes to choosing where to stay in Taipei

City, there are several popular areas that offer their own unique attractions and experiences.

Xinyi District

Located in the heart of Taipei City, Xinyi District is the city's central business and financial district. It's also home to many luxury hotels and high-end shopping centers, making it a great area to stay in if you're looking for a more upscale experience. The area is best known for its iconic landmark Taipei 101, a towering skyscraper that offers stunning views of the city. Other popular attractions in Xinyi District include the Taipei World Trade Center, Sun Yat-Sen Memorial Hall, and the Elephant Mountain hiking trail. The district also has a wide range of restaurants, bars, and nightclubs, making it a great place to experience Taipei City's vibrant nightlife.

Zhongzheng District

Located in the heart of Taipei City, Zhongzheng District is home to many of the city's cultural and historical attractions. It's a great area to stay in if you're interested in history and culture. The district is home to the Chiang Kai-Shek Memorial Hall, a landmark that commemorates the former President of the Republic of China. Other popular attractions in Zhongzheng District include the National Museum of History, the National Theater and Concert Hall, and the 228 Peace Memorial Park. The district also has a wide range of restaurants and cafes serving up traditional Taiwanese cuisine.

Da'an District

Located in eastern Taipei City, Da'an District is known for its vibrant nightlife, trendy cafes, and boutique shops. It's a great area to stay in if you're looking for a more lively and youthful atmosphere. The district is home to the popular shopping district of Zhongxiao Dunhua, which is filled with department stores, boutiques, and restaurants. Other popular attractions in Da'an District include Da'an Forest Park, Taipei Municipal Stadium, and the Taipei City Zoo. The district is also home to many universities, giving it a vibrant and youthful atmosphere.

Wanhua District

Located in western Taipei City, Wanhua District is the oldest district in the city and is known for its traditional markets, temples, and historical sites. It's a great area to stay in if you're interested in experiencing Taipei's traditional culture. The district is home to the iconic Longshan Temple, a beautiful temple that dates back to the 18th century. Other popular attractions in Wanhua District include the Huaxi Street Night Market, the Red House Theater, and the Bopiliao Historic Block. The district also has a wide range of traditional restaurants and food stalls serving up delicious Taiwanese street food.

Overall, each of these popular areas in Taipei City offer their own unique attractions and experiences, making them great options for travelers looking to explore this vibrant and exciting city.

Top Hotels And Hostels In Taipei City

Taipei City is home to a wide range of accommodation options, including luxurious hotels and affordable hostels. Here are some of the top hotels and hostels in Taipei City:

Grand Hyatt Taipei

Located in the heart of Taipei's Xinyi District, the Grand Hyatt Taipei is one of the city's most luxurious hotels. It boasts stunning views of Taipei 101, and is just a short walk from some of the city's top shopping and dining destinations. The hotel offers a range of rooms and suites, all of which are elegantly designed and feature modern amenities. Guests can also enjoy a variety of on-site restaurants and bars, including the renowned Yun Jin Chinese restaurant.

W Taipei

The W Taipei is a trendy and modern hotel located in the bustling Xinyi District. It's known for its stylish and colorful decor, as well as its high-end amenities and services. The hotel's rooms and suites are spacious and well-appointed, and feature floor-to-ceiling windows with stunning views of the city. The W Taipei also offers a range of on-site dining options, including the Michelin-starred restaurant, The Kitchen Table.

Flip Flop Hostel

The Flip Flop Hostel is a popular option for budget travelers and backpackers. Located in the Ximending District, it offers clean and comfortable dorm rooms and private rooms at an affordable price. The hostel also features a cozy lounge area where guests can relax and socialize, as well as a rooftop terrace with views of the city.

Homey Hostel

The Homey Hostel is another great option for budget travelers, located in the Da'an District. It offers a friendly and social atmosphere, with private and shared rooms available. The hostel is known for its clean and cozy rooms, as well as its helpful and knowledgeable staff. Guests can also enjoy a variety of on-site amenities, including a shared kitchen and lounge area.

Mandarin Oriental Taipei

The Mandarin Oriental Taipei is one of the most luxurious hotels in the city, located in the Da'an District. It boasts elegant and spacious rooms and suites, each designed with a unique blend of contemporary and traditional elements. The hotel also offers a range of on-site amenities, including a world-class spa, fitness center, and several dining options.

Overall, Taipei City has a range of accommodation options to suit all budgets and preferences. It doesn't matter if you're looking for a luxurious hotel or an affordable hostel, you're sure to find the perfect place to stay in this vibrant and exciting city.

CHAPTER FIVE

SIGHTSEEING IN TAIPEI CITY

Taipei City is a city that's full of fascinating sights and attractions that will keep any traveler busy for days. From cultural landmarks to beautiful natural scenery, there is something for everyone in this vibrant city. Here are some of the top tourist attractions and hidden gems that you should visit while in Taipei City

Top tourist attractions in Taipei City

National Palace Museum

he National Palace Museum is one of the top tourist attractions in Taipei City and is a must-visit for anyone interested in Chinese history and culture. Here's a comprehensive guide to the museum:

OVERVIEW
The National Palace Museum is located in the Shilin District of Taipei City and houses one of the world's largest collections of Chinese art and artifacts. It was originally founded in 1925 and moved to its current location in 1965. The museum has over

700,000 pieces in its collection, including ancient bronze ware, calligraphy, paintings, and ceramics, and is considered one of the most important museums in the world.

HISTORY
The National Palace Museum's collection is largely composed of artifacts that were once housed in the Forbidden City in Beijing. These artifacts were taken to Taiwan by the Kuomintang (KMT) during the Chinese Civil War, as a way to preserve China's cultural heritage. The collection was moved to Taiwan in 1949 and has been housed in the National Palace Museum ever since.

COLLECTIONS
The museum's collection is divided into several categories, including ceramics, jades, bronzes, calligraphy, and paintings. Some of the most famous pieces in the collection include:

Jadeite Cabbage: This small jade sculpture of a cabbage and a grasshopper is one of the most famous pieces in the museum's collection. It's considered a national treasure of Taiwan and is often used as a symbol of the museum.

Meat-shaped Stone: This is a piece of jasper that's been carved to look like a piece of braised pork. It's considered a masterpiece of Qing Dynasty art and is one of the most popular pieces in the museum's collection.

Bronze Wine Vessel in the Shape of a Rhinoceros: This is a bronze wine vessel from the Shang Dynasty that's been cast in the shape of a rhinoceros. It's one of the oldest pieces in the museum's collection and is considered a masterpiece of early Chinese bronze work.

Along the River During the Qingming Festival: This is a scroll painting from the Song Dynasty that's over 17 feet long. It depicts daily life in China during the Qingming Festival and is considered one of the most important works of Chinese art.

EXHIBITIONS
The National Palace Museum has several permanent exhibitions that showcase its collection, as well as temporary exhibitions that feature rotating pieces from the collection. Some of the permanent exhibitions include:

Gallery of Jadeite Cabbage and Meat-shaped Stone: This gallery features two of the most famous pieces in the museum's collection, the Jadeite Cabbage and the Meat-shaped Stone.

Gallery of Bronzes: This gallery features a collection of over 400 bronze artifacts from the Shang and Zhou Dynasties.

Gallery of Calligraphy and Painting: This gallery features a collection of over 10,000 calligraphy and painting works, including pieces from famous Chinese artists such as Su Shi and Zhang Daqian.

Tips For Visiting

Purchase tickets in advance: The National Palace Museum is a popular tourist attraction and can get very crowded, especially during peak season. To avoid waiting in long lines, it's a good idea to purchase tickets in advance online or through your hotel.

Allow plenty of time: The museum is huge and it's easy to spend several hours exploring its collections. Plan to spend at least half a day at the museum to see the highlights of the collection.

Take a guided tour: The museum offers guided tours in English and other languages, which can be a great way to learn more about the collection and its history.

Check the opening hours: The museum is closed on Mondays, and has limited opening hours on Tuesdays, so make sure to check the opening hours before planning your visit.

Don't miss the special exhibitions: In addition to its permanent collection, the National Palace Museum also hosts special exhibitions throughout the year. Check the museum's website for information about upcoming exhibitions.

Rent an audio guide: The museum offers audio guides in several languages, which can provide helpful information about the pieces in the collection.

Wear comfortable shoes: The museum is quite large and requires a lot of walking, so make sure to wear comfortable shoes.

Bring a water bottle and snacks: There are several cafes and restaurants on the museum grounds, but they can get crowded during peak hours. To avoid long lines, it's a good idea to bring your own water bottle and snacks.

GETTING THERE
The National Palace Museum is located in the Shilin District of Taipei City, and can be reached by several methods of transportation:

MRT: Take the Red Line to Shilin Station, and then take a bus to the museum.

Taxi: Taxis are widely available in Taipei City and can take you directly to the museum.

In conclusion, the National Palace Museum is one of Taipei City's top tourist attractions and is a must-visit for anyone interested in Chinese history and culture. With its vast collection of artifacts, beautiful galleries, and informative guided tours, the museum is sure to provide a memorable experience for visitors of all ages.

Taipei 101

Taipei 101 is an iconic skyscraper located in the Xinyi District of Taipei City. It was completed in 2004 and was once the tallest building in the world until it was surpassed by the Burj Khalifa in Dubai. Today, it's still one of the tallest buildings in the world and a must-visit attraction for anyone traveling to Taipei City.

HISTORY AND DESIGN OF TAIPEI 101

The idea for Taipei 101 was first proposed in 1997 as a response to the Asian financial crisis. The goal was to create a new landmark for Taipei City that would help boost the economy and showcase Taiwan's technological prowess.

The building's design is inspired by traditional Chinese architecture and features elements like pagoda-style roofs and bamboo-shaped columns. It also incorporates modern engineering and sustainable design principles, such as a tuned mass damper that helps the building withstand earthquakes and high winds.

What To See And Do At Taipei 101

Observation Deck: The Taipei 101 observation deck is located on the 89th floor of the building and offers panoramic views of the city. Visitors can take an express elevator that travels at 37 miles per hour and reach the observation deck in just 37 seconds. Once there, they can take in the stunning views and learn more about the building's design and construction.

Shopping and Dining: Taipei 101 is home to a world-class mall that features luxury shops, restaurants, and cafes. Visitors can find everything from designer fashion to Taiwanese souvenirs and enjoy a meal or coffee break while taking in the view.

Light Shows: Taipei 101 is also known for its dazzling light shows that are displayed on the building's exterior. The shows are synchronized with music and are a popular attraction in Taipei City, especially during holidays and special events.

Tips For Visiting Taipei 101

Buy Tickets in Advance: The Taipei 101 observation deck can get very crowded, especially during peak season. To avoid waiting in long lines, it's a good idea to purchase tickets in advance online or through your hotel.

Time Your Visit: Taipei 101 is beautiful at any time of day, but the best time to visit is during sunset or at night when the city lights up. Consider planning your visit accordingly to get the best views.

Dress Appropriately: The observation deck can be quite chilly, so it's a good idea to bring a jacket or sweater. Additionally, visitors should dress appropriately for a formal setting when visiting the mall or restaurants.

Take Public Transportation: Taipei 101 is located in the Xinyi District of Taipei City and is easily accessible by subway. Taking public transportation is much more convenient and cost-effective than taking a taxi, especially during rush hour.

Chiang Kai-Shek Memorial Hall

The Chiang Kai-Shek Memorial Hall is one of the most famous landmarks in Taipei City. It was built in honor of the former President of the Republic of China, Chiang Kai-Shek, who led the country from 1949 until his death in 1975. The memorial hall is located in the heart of Taipei City and is surrounded by a large park that's a popular spot for locals and tourists alike.

History of the Memorial Hall

The construction of the Chiang Kai-Shek Memorial Hall began in 1976, shortly after Chiang's death. It took six years to complete and was officially opened to the public in 1980. The memorial hall is designed in the style of traditional Chinese architecture and features a grand white building with blue-tiled roofs.

Inside the memorial hall, visitors can find a museum dedicated to Chiang's life and achievements. The museum houses many artifacts related to Chiang's military career and political legacy, including his personal belongings, photographs, and documents.

Highlights of the Memorial Hall

Changing of the Guard Ceremony: One of the most popular attractions at the Chiang Kai-Shek Memorial Hall is the changing of the guard ceremony. The ceremony takes place every hour on the hour and features soldiers dressed in traditional uniforms performing a highly choreographed routine.

National Concert Hall and National Theater: The Chiang Kai-Shek Memorial Hall is also home to the National Concert Hall and National Theater, which are both located on either side of the memorial hall. The National Concert Hall is a world-class performance venue that hosts concerts and other cultural events throughout the year. The National Theater is a beautiful theater that features performances of traditional Chinese opera and other cultural shows.

Views of Taipei City: Visitors can climb to the top of the memorial hall to get stunning views of Taipei City. The observation deck offers panoramic views of the city skyline and is a great place to take photos.

Cultural Events: The Chiang Kai-Shek Memorial Hall is also a popular venue for cultural events and festivals. Visitors can check the event schedule to see if there are any upcoming events during their visit.

Tips For Visiting The Memorial Hall

Dress Appropriately: The Chiang Kai-Shek Memorial Hall is a solemn and respectful site, so visitors should dress appropriately. Avoid wearing shorts, tank tops, or other revealing clothing.

Be Respectful: Visitors should also be respectful while inside the memorial hall and refrain from talking loudly or making excessive noise. Remember that this is a place of solemnity and reverence.

Watch the Changing of the Guard Ceremony: The changing of the guard ceremony is a must-see attraction at the Chiang Kai-Shek Memorial Hall. Visitors should make sure to arrive a few minutes before the ceremony starts to secure a good viewing spot.

Explore the Park: The park surrounding the memorial hall is a beautiful place to relax and take a stroll. Visitors can see the large bronze statue of Chiang Kai-Shek, walk through the garden of Chinese plants, and see the elegant Taiwan Democracy Memorial Wall.

The Chiang Kai-Shek Memorial Hall is a significant cultural and historical landmark in Taipei City that's definitely worth a visit. If you're interested in history, culture, or just want to take in the stunning views of the city, the memorial hall has something to offer for everyone.

Taipei Zoo

Taipei Zoo is the largest zoo in Asia and one of the most popular tourist attractions in Taipei City. The zoo is home to over 4,000 animals from more than 400 different species, making it a must-visit destination for animal lovers.

HISTORY AND OVERVIEW OF TAIPEI ZOO

Taipei Zoo was first established in 1914 during the Japanese colonial era and was originally called the "New Park". After World War II, the zoo was renamed the Taipei Zoo and became a public facility managed by the Taipei City Government.

Today, Taipei Zoo covers an area of 165 hectares and is divided into several themed areas, including the Formosan Animal Area, the Children's Zoo, the Amphibian and Reptile House, the Bird World, the African Animal Area, and the Asian Tropical Rainforest Area.

ANIMAL HIGHLIGHTS AT TAIPEI ZOO

Giant Pandas: One of the most popular exhibits at Taipei Zoo is the Giant Panda House, which is home to two giant pandas, Tuan Tuan and Yuan Yuan. The pandas were a gift from the Chinese government to Taiwan in 2008 and have since become beloved symbols of the zoo. Unfortunately, one of the panda is dead.

African Animals: The African Animal Area is home to a variety of animals from the savannas and jungles of Africa, including giraffes, zebras, cheetahs, and lions. Visitors can also see the zoo's African elephants, which are a rare and endangered species.

Formosan Animals: The Formosan Animal Area is dedicated to animals that are native to Taiwan, including the Formosan black bear, the Mikado pheasant, and the Formosan sika deer. Visitors can learn about these unique and endangered animals and the efforts to conserve them.

Children's Zoo: The Children's Zoo is a popular area for families with young children. It features a petting zoo where kids can interact with domestic animals, as well as exhibits on farm animals and insects.

Activities And Programs At Taipei Zoo

In addition to viewing the animal exhibits, Taipei Zoo offers a variety of activities and programs for visitors, including:

Animal feeding and interactions: Visitors can purchase food to feed some of the animals, such as the giraffes and elephants. There are also opportunities to interact with some of the animals under the supervision of zoo staff.

Night Safari: Taipei Zoo offers a nighttime guided tour where visitors can see the animals in a different light. The tour is available on weekends and holidays and requires advance reservations.

Zoo education programs: Taipei Zoo offers educational programs for visitors of all ages, including guided tours, workshops, and lectures. These programs are designed to teach visitors about the animals and their habitats, as well as the importance of conservation.

Tips For Visiting Taipei Zoo

Wear comfortable clothing and shoes: Taipei Zoo is a large and hilly park, so it's important to wear comfortable shoes and clothing.

Bring sunscreen and water: Taipei can be very hot and humid, so it's important to stay hydrated and protect yourself from the sun.

Visit early or late in the day: Taipei Zoo can get very crowded during peak hours, so it's best to visit early in the morning or late in the day to avoid the crowds.

Be respectful: Visitors should be respectful of the animals and their habitats, and should not attempt to feed or touch them without the guidance of zoo staff.

GETTING TO TAIPEI ZOO

Taipei Zoo is located in the Wenshan District of Taipei City, and is easily accessible by public transportation.

MRT: The Muzha Line of Taipei's Metro system has a stop right outside the zoo's entrance. The station is called "Taipei Zoo Station" and is located at the southern end of the line.

Bus: There are several bus routes that stop near Taipei Zoo

ADMISSION AND HOURS

Admission to Taipei Zoo is at a fixed price The zoo is open from 9:00 am to 5:00 pm daily, with extended hours until 6:00 pm on weekends and holidays.

In conclusion, Taipei Zoo is a wonderful destination for animal lovers and families with children. With its wide variety of animal exhibits and interactive programs, visitors can learn about the unique and endangered animals of Taiwan and the world. As one of the largest and most popular zoos in Asia, Taipei Zoo is definitely worth a visit when exploring Taipei City.

Hidden Gems In Taipei City

Taipei City is not only home to popular tourist attractions, but also hidden gems waiting to be discovered. These places offer unique experiences that are off the beaten path, and they are often beloved by locals and savvy travelers. Here are some hidden gems in Taipei City worth exploring:

Beitou Hot Springs

Beitou is a district in Taipei City that's known for its hot springs. The hot springs are located in a beautiful natural setting, surrounded by mountains and lush vegetation. Visitors can soak in the hot springs and enjoy the scenic beauty of the area. Beitou is easily accessible by MRT, and there are many hot spring resorts, public hot spring baths, and private hot spring rooms to choose from.

Ximending

Ximending is a popular shopping and entertainment district in Taipei City that's often called the "Harajuku of Taipei". It's a lively area filled with street performers, food vendors, and shops selling everything from fashion to electronics. Ximending is a great place to experience the vibrant youth culture of Taipei, and there are many hidden alleys and streets that are worth exploring.

Longshan Temple

Longshan Temple is a beautiful and historic temple in Taipei City that's over 300 years old. It's one of the city's most popular temples and is known for its ornate decorations and beautiful architecture. However, the temple also has a hidden gem called the Dragon and Tiger Pagodas, which are located behind the main temple. The pagodas are surrounded by a lotus pond and are decorated with intricate carvings and paintings.

Elephant Mountain

Elephant Mountain is a popular hiking trail in Taipei City that offers stunning views of the city skyline. The hike is relatively easy and takes about 20-30 minutes to reach the top. It's a great place to watch the sunset and take photos. However, there's a hidden gem at the base of the mountain called the Xiangshan Visitor Center. The visitor center is a small museum that showcases the history and ecology of the area, and it's also a great place to get information about the hiking trail and the surrounding area.

Jiufen

Jiufen is a small town located about an hour outside of Taipei City. It's a hidden gem that's often compared to the setting of the famous Japanese animated film, "Spirited Away". The town is built on the side of a mountain and is known for its narrow alleys, red lanterns, and beautiful views of the ocean. Visitors can explore the town's many tea houses, souvenir shops, and temples, and soak in the town's unique atmosphere.

Daan Forest Park
Daan Forest Park is a beautiful park located in the heart of Taipei City. It's a hidden gem that's often overlooked by tourists, but beloved by locals. The park is home to a large lake, walking paths, and many beautiful trees and flowers. It's a great place to relax and enjoy nature, and there are often events and festivals held in the park throughout the year.

Overall, Taipei City is a treasure trove of hidden gems waiting to be explored. These places offer unique experiences and are often beloved by locals. By venturing off the beaten path and exploring these hidden gems, travelers can gain a deeper understanding and appreciation of Taipei City and its culture.

Tips For Visiting Taipei City's Tourist Attractions

Purchase Tickets in Advance: Many of Taipei City's top tourist attractions can get very crowded, especially during peak season. To avoid waiting in long lines, it's a good idea to purchase tickets in advance online or through your hotel. Most attractions offer discounted tickets online or bundled packages that include multiple attractions, which can save you time and money.

[84]

Use Public Transportation: Taipei City has a well-developed public transportation system that includes buses, subways, and trains. It's easy to get around the city using public transportation, and it's much cheaper than taking taxis. The MRT (subway) system is especially convenient, as it connects to most of the major attractions in the city. You can purchase an EasyCard at any MRT station or convenience store, which is a reloadable smart card that can be used to pay for fares on all forms of public transportation.

Plan Your Time Wisely: Taipei City has so many great attractions that it can be difficult to see them all in one trip. To make the most of your time, plan your itinerary in advance and prioritize the attractions that you most want to see. Consider grouping attractions by location to save time on transportation, or consider booking a guided tour to get the most out of your visit.

Be Respectful: When visiting temples and other cultural landmarks in Taipei City, it's important to be respectful of local customs and traditions. Dress modestly, remove your shoes when entering temples, and be mindful of your behavior. Don't touch or climb on historic structures, and avoid taking flash photography in areas where it's prohibited. Additionally, be mindful of the environment by disposing of trash properly and avoiding behaviors that could harm the natural environment.

Try Local Food: Taipei City is known for its delicious street food and night markets. Don't be afraid to try new things, and be adventurous with your food choices. Some of the most popular Taiwanese dishes include beef noodle soup, stinky tofu, and bubble tea. If you're not sure where to start, ask locals for recommendations or consider booking a food tour.

Stay Safe: Taipei City is generally a safe place to visit, but it's important to take precautions to ensure your safety. Be aware of your surroundings and avoid carrying large amounts of cash or valuables. Keep your belongings close to you at all times, especially in crowded areas. If you're traveling alone or at night, consider taking a taxi or using a ride-hailing app like Uber or Grab. Finally, be sure to stay hydrated and wear sunscreen during the hot summer months.

Learn Basic Mandarin: While many people in Taipei City speak English, it can still be helpful to learn some basic Mandarin phrases before your trip. Not only will this help you communicate with locals, but it can also make ordering food and navigating public transportation easier. Some basic phrases to learn include "ni hao" (hello), "xiexie" (thank you), and "zaijian" (goodbye).

Check the Weather: Taipei City has a subtropical climate with hot, humid summers and mild winters. It's important to check the weather forecast before your trip so that you can pack accordingly. During the summer months, be sure to bring lightweight, breathable clothing and a hat to protect yourself from the sun. During the winter months, you may need a light jacket or sweater.

Be Prepared for Crowds: Taipei City is a popular tourist destination, and many of its attractions can get very crowded, especially during peak season. Be prepared for long lines and crowds, and consider visiting popular attractions during off-peak hours. Additionally, be prepared to wait in line for popular street food stalls and restaurants.

Respect Local Customs: Taiwanese culture is rich with customs and traditions that may be unfamiliar to visitors. Take the time to learn about local customs and etiquette, and be respectful of them during your visit. For example, it's customary to offer a small donation when visiting temples, and it's considered impolite to point with your finger. By respecting local customs, you'll show that you're interested in learning about the local culture and will have a more enjoyable experience during your trip.

In summary, by following these tips for visiting Taipei City's tourist attractions, you can have a safe and enjoyable trip while making the most of your time in this vibrant and exciting city.

CHAPTER SIX

FOOD AND DRINK IN TAIPEI CITY

Taiwanese cuisine is known for its unique blend of flavors, influenced by Chinese, Japanese, and indigenous Taiwanese culinary traditions. Taipei City, being the capital city of Taiwan, is a food lover's paradise with countless dining options, ranging from street food to Michelin-starred restaurants.

Taiwanese Cuisine

Taiwanese cuisine is a reflection of the country's unique history and cultural heritage. It combines elements of Chinese, Japanese, and indigenous Taiwanese cuisine, resulting in a vibrant and diverse culinary scene. Taiwanese cuisine is known for its bold flavors, use of fresh ingredients, and attention to texture.

One of the most popular dishes in Taiwanese cuisine is beef noodle soup, which is considered a national dish. This hearty soup is made with tender beef, noodles, and an array of spices and herbs, including garlic, star anise, and Sichuan peppercorns. Other popular noodle dishes include dan dan noodles, which are spicy noodles with ground pork and peanut sauce, and zha jiang mian, which are noodles served with a savory sauce made with fermented soybeans.

Another iconic dish in Taiwanese cuisine is xiao long bao, also known as soup dumplings. These small steamed buns are filled with juicy meat and savory soup, making them a popular street food snack. Other popular street food snacks in Taiwan include scallion pancakes, which are crispy and flaky pancakes made with scallions and sesame oil, and stinky tofu, a pungent fermented tofu that is either deep-fried or served in a hot pot.

Taiwanese cuisine also features a variety of seafood dishes, including oyster omelets, which are made with eggs, oysters, and starch, and seafood congee, which is a comforting rice porridge made with a variety of seafood. Taiwanese cuisine is also known for its use of a variety of meats, including pork, chicken, and duck. One popular dish is three-cup chicken, which is made with chicken, garlic, ginger, and basil, and cooked with soy sauce, rice wine, and sesame oil.

For those with a sweet tooth, Taiwanese cuisine has a range of desserts and snacks to choose from. One of the most popular Taiwanese desserts is shaved ice, which is a refreshing dessert made with shaved ice, fresh fruit, condensed milk, and syrup. Other popular desserts include pineapple cakes, which are buttery pastries filled with pineapple jam, and mochi, which are chewy rice cakes filled with sweet bean paste.

Some of the most popular Taiwanese dishes include:

Beef noodle soup: A hearty soup made with tender beef, noodles, and an array of spices and herbs.

Bubble tea: A Taiwanese invention that has become a global phenomenon, bubble tea is a tea-based drink that comes with chewy tapioca pearls or fruit jelly.

Xiao Long Bao: Also known as soup dumplings, these are small steamed buns filled with juicy meat and savory soup.

Scallion pancakes: A crispy and flaky pancake made with scallions and sesame oil.

Stinky tofu: A pungent fermented tofu that is either deep-fried or served in a hot pot.

Oyster omelet: A popular Taiwanese street food made with eggs, oysters, and starch.

In addition to its iconic dishes, Taiwanese cuisine also features a variety of teas. Taiwan is known for its high-quality teas, including oolong tea and black tea. Tea shops can be found all over Taipei City, and they offer a wide range of tea varieties and flavors.

Overall, Taiwanese cuisine is a unique and flavorful blend of different culinary traditions. Taipei City is the perfect place to explore this diverse cuisine, with its countless dining options ranging from street food to high-end restaurants.

Famous food and drink in Taipei City

Taipei City is renowned for its food culture, and there are many iconic dishes and beverages that visitors should try when in the city. Here are some of the must-try food and drinks in Taipei City:

Shilin Night Market
Shilin Night Market is one of the most popular night markets in Taipei City, and it is known for its street food. Visitors can find an array of snacks and dishes such as stinky tofu, fried chicken, grilled squid, and Taiwanese sausages. The market also offers a variety of drinks such as bubble tea, fruit juices, and freshly brewed tea.

Din Tai Fung

Din Tai Fung is a Michelin-starred restaurant chain that originated in Taipei City and is famous for its xiao long bao, or soup dumplings. The restaurant's xiao long bao has thin skin, a delicate filling, and a savory soup inside. Din Tai Fung now has locations all around the world, but the original branch in Taipei City is a must-visit for foodies.

Yongkang Beef Noodle

Yongkang Beef Noodle is a restaurant that specializes in beef noodle soup, which is considered one of the most iconic Taiwanese dishes. The restaurant's broth is slow-cooked for hours with beef bones and an array of spices and herbs, resulting in a rich and flavorful soup. The noodles are cooked al dente, and the beef is tender and flavorful. The restaurant also offers other Taiwanese dishes such as scallion pancakes and oyster omelets.

Mango shaved ice

Mango shaved ice is a refreshing dessert that is perfect for the hot and humid weather in Taipei City. The dessert is made with shaved ice, fresh mango, condensed milk, and syrup. The shaved ice is finely shaved, resulting in a fluffy and light texture, and the mango is sweet and juicy. Visitors can find mango shaved ice in many dessert shops and cafes in Taipei City.

e) Gua bao

Gua bao, also known as Taiwanese-style hamburger, is a sandwich made with fluffy steamed buns, braised pork belly, and pickled vegetables. The pork belly is cooked with soy sauce, sugar, and an array of spices and herbs, resulting in tender and flavorful meat. The pickled vegetables add a refreshing and tangy flavor to the sandwich. Gua bao can be found in many restaurants and night markets in Taipei City.

Taiwanese tea
Taiwan is known for its high-quality teas, such as oolong tea and black tea. Tea shops can be found all over Taipei City, and they offer a wide range of tea varieties and flavors. Visitors can enjoy a cup of hot tea in a traditional tea house or try a refreshing bubble tea with tapioca pearls or fruit jelly.

Overall, Taipei City's food and drink scene offers a diverse range of flavors and experiences for visitors. From street food to high-end restaurants, there's something for every taste and budget.

Night Markets And Street Food

Night markets and street food are an integral part of the food and drink scene in Taipei City, offering a wide range of cheap, delicious, and authentic Taiwanese cuisine.

Shilin Night Market

Shilin Night Market is the largest and most famous night market in Taipei City, attracting both locals and tourists. The market is famous for its wide variety of street food, including fried chicken, grilled squid, oyster omelets, stinky tofu, and bubble tea. In addition to street food, the market also has a shopping area where visitors can find souvenirs, clothes, and accessories.

Raohe Night Market

Raohe Night Market is located in the Songshan District and is known for its traditional Taiwanese snacks. Some of the must-try dishes at Raohe Night Market include pork pepper buns, beef noodles, and black pepper buns. The market is also known for its lively atmosphere and street performances.

Ningxia Night Market

Ningxia Night Market is one of the oldest night markets in Taipei City, dating back to the 1950s. The market is known for its seafood and meat dishes, such as grilled squid, oyster omelets, and pork intestine soup. Ningxia Night Market also has a section dedicated to Taiwanese sweets and desserts, such as shaved ice and mochi.

Huaxi Night Market (Snake Alley)

Huaxi Night Market, also known as Snake Alley, is a controversial night market that is famous for its exotic food, including snake meat and blood.

However, in recent years, the market has shifted its focus towards more mainstream Taiwanese cuisine, such as stinky tofu, oyster omelets, and Taiwanese sausage.

Tonghua Night Market
Tonghua Night Market is located in the Da'an District and is known for its fusion cuisine, combining Taiwanese and Japanese flavors. Some of the must-try dishes at Tonghua Night Market include Japanese-style grilled eel, takoyaki (octopus balls), and Taiwanese-style fried chicken.

Ningxia Night Market
Ningxia Night Market is one of the oldest night markets in Taipei City, dating back to the 1950s. The market is known for its seafood and meat dishes, such as grilled squid, oyster omelets, and pork intestine soup. Ningxia Night Market also has a section dedicated to Taiwanese sweets and desserts, such as shaved ice and mochi.

Ximending Night Market
Ximending Night Market is located in the Wanhua District and is known for its trendy fashion and street food. The market is popular with young people and has a wide variety of street food, including crispy chicken, pork ribs, and fried noodles.

Liaoning Night Market

Liaoning Night Market is located in the Zhongshan District and is known for its spicy food. Some of the must-try dishes at Liaoning Night Market include spicy hot pot, spicy duck blood, and spicy crayfish. The market also has a section dedicated to Taiwanese sweets and desserts.

Taipei City's night markets and street food scene offer a unique culinary experience, where visitors can sample a wide range of authentic Taiwanese cuisine in a vibrant and lively atmosphere. From the famous Shilin Night Market to the exotic Huaxi Night Market, Taipei City's night markets and street food have something to offer for everyone.

Restaurants and cafes

Taipei City is a food lover's paradise, with an abundance of restaurants and cafes catering to all tastes and budgets. From Michelin-starred restaurants to trendy cafes, here are some of the best places to dine in Taipei City:

RAW: This Michelin-starred restaurant is known for its innovative Taiwanese cuisine, using locally sourced ingredients. The menu changes seasonally, and the dishes are beautifully presented. Some of the signature dishes include the abalone with lobster roe and the foie gras with smoked eel.

MUME: Another Michelin-starred restaurant, MUME combines Taiwanese and European cuisine to create dishes that are both creative and delicious. The restaurant has a relaxed atmosphere, and the menu changes frequently, depending on the availability of seasonal ingredients.

Addiction Aquatic Development: This seafood market is a popular dining destination in Taipei City. The market features a sushi bar, seafood grill, and wine bar. The sushi is made with fresh, high-quality seafood, and the grilled seafood is cooked to perfection.

Din Tai Fung: No list of Taipei City's best restaurants would be complete without mentioning Din Tai Fung. This famous restaurant chain is known for its xiao long bao (soup dumplings), which are filled with juicy meat and savory soup. The restaurant has several locations in Taipei City, and it's always busy, so be prepared to wait in line.

Shin Yeh: This upscale restaurant serves classic Taiwanese dishes in a stylish setting. The menu features dishes such as stir-fried noodles with seafood, Taiwanese-style beef stew, and stir-fried bamboo shoots. The restaurant also has a great selection of Taiwanese teas and local beers.

La Mesa: This restaurant serves contemporary Taiwanese cuisine in a cozy and intimate setting. The menu changes seasonally and features dishes made with local and organic ingredients. Some of the must-try dishes include the beef tartare with

Taiwanese guava and the grilled squid with lemongrass and chili.

Fika Fika Café: This specialty coffee shop serves high-quality coffee and pastries. The café has a Scandinavian-inspired interior and a relaxing atmosphere, making it a great place to hang out and catch up with friends.

Ice Monster: This dessert café specializes in shaved ice, a popular Taiwanese dessert. The shaved ice is topped with fresh fruit, condensed milk, and syrup, making it a refreshing treat on a hot day.

Chen San Ding: This tiny stall in the Shida Night Market is famous for its crispy milk crepe, a popular Taiwanese street food. The crepe is filled with a sweet and creamy filling and is cooked to perfection on a griddle.

Kao Chi: This restaurant serves classic Shanghai-style cuisine, including xiao long bao, pan-fried dumplings, and scallion pancakes. The restaurant has a traditional Chinese décor and a bustling atmosphere, making it a great place to experience authentic Chinese cuisine.

If you're looking for a fine dining experience or a casual meal, Taipei City has something for everyone. With so many great restaurants and cafes to choose from, you'll never run out of options to satisfy your culinary cravings.

Food Tours And Cooking Classes

If you're interested in learning more about Taiwanese cuisine and want to try your hand at cooking it yourself, there are plenty of food tours and cooking classes available in Taipei City. These experiences allow you to immerse yourself in the local food culture and learn from expert chefs. Some popular food tours and cooking classes include:

Taipei Eats Food Tour: This guided food tour takes you to some of Taipei City's most famous food markets and restaurants, where you can taste a variety of dishes and learn about the city's culinary history.

Taipei Cooking Class: This cooking class is led by a professional Taiwanese chef who will teach you how to make traditional dishes such as beef noodle soup and steamed dumplings.

Taipei Tea Culture Experience: This experience takes you to a traditional tea house, where you can learn about the history and culture of Taiwanese tea and participate in a tea-making ceremony.

Dietary Restrictions

If you have dietary restrictions or preferences, Taipei City has plenty of options for you as well. Many restaurants and cafes offer vegetarian and vegan options, and some even specialize in plant-based cuisine. Gluten-free options are also becoming more common in Taipei City. If you have any specific dietary requirements, it's best to do some research ahead of time to find restaurants that cater to your needs.

Overall, Taipei City is a food lover's paradise, with something for everyone. From traditional Taiwanese dishes to international cuisine, from street food to Michelin-starred restaurants, Taipei City has it all. It doesn't matter if you're a foodie or just looking to try some new flavors, Taipei City is sure to delight your taste buds.

CHAPTER SEVEN

SHOPPING IN TAIPEI CITY

Taipei City is a shopper's paradise, offering an eclectic mix of shopping experiences that cater to every taste and budget. From luxury shopping malls to bustling street markets, Taipei City has something for everyone.

In this chapter, we will explore the popular shopping districts, best shopping malls, and unique souvenirs to buy in Taipei City.

Popular Shopping Districts In Taipei City

Xinyi District

The Xinyi District is one of the most upscale and fashionable areas in Taipei City, and it's a top destination for luxury shopping. The district is home to the famous Taipei 101 skyscraper, which boasts a world-class shopping mall, and Breeze Xinyi, a trendy shopping complex that features an eclectic mix of fashion, food, and entertainment. There are also several designer flagship stores in the district, including Louis Vuitton, Gucci, Chanel, and Dior. For those looking for more affordable options, the district also has a number of department stores such as Mitsukoshi and ATT 4 Fun, which offer a variety of brands and products.

Zhongxiao Dunhua

The Zhongxiao Dunhua area is a popular shopping district for younger shoppers who are looking for unique and stylish clothing and accessories. The area is known for its independent boutiques and designer stores, which offer one-of-a-kind pieces that you can't find anywhere else.

One of the most popular destinations in the district is Eslite Spectrum, a multi-level bookstore and retail complex that features a wide range of products, including books, music, fashion, and beauty. Another popular destination is the Wufenpu Wholesale Market, which is one of the largest clothing wholesale markets in Asia and is a great place to find affordable clothing and accessories. For those looking for more traditional shopping experiences, SOGO Department Store is a good option, offering a wide variety of products from luxury brands to more affordable options.

Shilin Night Market

Shilin Night Market is the largest and most famous night market in Taipei City and is a must-visit destination for anyone who loves shopping and street food. The market is known for its vibrant atmosphere and endless stalls selling everything from clothing and accessories to souvenirs and food. Some of the popular items you can find at Shilin Night Market include Taiwanese-style clothing, shoes, bags, and jewelry, as well as traditional Taiwanese snacks and drinks like oyster omelets, stinky tofu, and bubble tea. Visitors should be prepared to haggle with vendors and try lots of new foods while exploring the market.

These popular shopping districts in Taipei City offer a diverse range of shopping experiences that cater to different interests and budgets. Whether you're looking for luxury fashion, unique boutiques, or street markets, Taipei City has something to offer for every type of shopper.

Best Shopping Malls In Taipei City

Taipei 101 Mall
The Taipei 101 Mall is one of the most iconic shopping destinations in Taipei City. Located in the Xinyi District, the mall is part of the Taipei 101

building, which was once the tallest building in the world. The mall features over 500 stores spread across five levels, including high-end designer boutiques, luxury department stores, and trendy fashion retailers.

The mall is anchored by two department stores, Shin Kong Mitsukoshi and Uni-President Hankyu Department Store, which offer a wide range of products including fashion, beauty, and home goods. In addition, the mall is home to several flagship stores, including Chanel, Louis Vuitton, and Gucci, making it a must-visit for luxury shoppers.

One of the highlights of the Taipei 101 Mall is its Food Court, which features a wide range of local and international cuisine. Visitors can sample everything from traditional Taiwanese snacks to Japanese ramen and Korean fried chicken.

Shin Kong Mitsukoshi
Shin Kong Mitsukoshi is a Japanese department store chain that has several locations throughout Taipei City. The stores offer a wide range of products, including fashion, beauty, home goods, and electronics.

The flagship store in the Xinyi District is one of the largest and most popular department stores in Taipei City. The store features several levels of shopping, including a luxury brand section, a beauty department, and a home goods section. The basement level of the store is dedicated to food, with a wide range of local and international cuisine available.

Shin Kong Mitsukoshi is known for its high-end products and excellent customer service. The store offers a VIP program for frequent shoppers, which includes special discounts and invitations to exclusive events.

Miramar Entertainment Park

Miramar Entertainment Park is a shopping mall and entertainment complex located in the Dazhi District. The mall features over 200 stores, a movie theater, and an amusement park.

One of the highlights of the Miramar Entertainment Park is its Ferris wheel, which offers stunning views of Taipei City. The mall also features several unique stores, including a store that specializes in retro video games and a store that sells Japanese goods.

In addition to shopping, the mall offers a wide range of entertainment options, including an arcade, a bowling alley, and a karaoke bar. The mall is also home to several restaurants, ranging from casual fast food to upscale dining.

Taipei City has several excellent shopping malls that offer a wide range of products and experiences.

From luxury shopping at the Taipei 101 Mall to the unique stores at Miramar Entertainment Park, there is something for every type of shopper in Taipei City.

Unique Souvenirs To Buy In Taipei City

Taipei City is home to a variety of unique souvenirs that are perfect for taking back home as a reminder of your trip. From delicious snacks to traditional handicrafts, there's something for everyone.

Pineapple Cakes: Pineapple cakes are one of the most popular souvenirs to buy in Taipei City. These small, bite-sized cakes are made with buttery pastry and filled with sweet pineapple jam. They are a perfect gift to take back home for friends and family or to enjoy yourself as a delicious snack. Some of the popular places to buy pineapple cakes include SunnyHills, Chia Te Bakery, and Kuo Yuan Ye.

Bubble Tea: Bubble tea is a Taiwanese invention that has become a global phenomenon. The drink is made with tea, milk, and chewy tapioca balls and is available in countless flavors and varieties. In Taipei City, there are numerous bubble tea shops where you can find this refreshing drink. Some of the popular places to buy bubble tea include Chun Shui Tang, 50 Lan, and Coco.

Taiwanese Tea: Taiwan is known for producing some of the highest quality tea in the world, and there are many tea shops throughout Taipei City that sell a wide variety of teas. Whether you're looking for oolong tea, black tea, green tea, or other types of tea, you're sure to find something that suits your taste. Some of the popular tea shops in Taipei City include Ten Ren Tea, Sun Moon Lake Tea, and Wistaria Tea House.

Handicrafts: Taipei City is also known for its traditional handicrafts, such as ceramics, paper umbrellas, and wooden sculptures. The Taipei Gift Center, located in the Xinyi District, is a great place to shop for these types of items. You can also find handmade pottery, silk products, and other traditional crafts at the various night markets in Taipei City, such as Shilin Night Market and Raohe Night Market.

Calligraphy Supplies: Calligraphy is a traditional art form that has been practiced in Taiwan for centuries. Taipei City is home to several shops that sell calligraphy supplies, including brushes, ink, and paper. Some of the popular places to buy calligraphy supplies include Eslite Spectrum and Wu Dao Tang.

Taiwanese Liquor: Taiwan is known for producing high-quality liquor, including whiskey, beer, and fruit wine. Some of the popular Taiwanese liquor brands include Kavalan Whiskey, Taiwan Beer, and Shaoxing Wine. These liquors are great souvenirs to take back home and share with friends and family.

Traditional Snacks: Taipei City is home to many traditional snacks that are perfect for taking back home as souvenirs. Some of the popular snacks include pork jerky, beef noodles, and stinky tofu. You can find these snacks at various night markets throughout Taipei City, such as Ningxia Night Market and Tonghua Night Market.

Handmade Soap: Handmade soap is a popular souvenir to buy in Taipei City. These soaps are made from natural ingredients and come in a variety of scents and designs. Some of the popular handmade soap brands in Taipei City include Herbaria, Soapapilla, and Lin Hsin Hsin.

Hakka Lei Cha: Hakka Lei Cha is a traditional Taiwanese dish that consists of ground tea leaves and a variety of vegetables, served over rice. It is a healthy and nutritious meal that is perfect for taking back home as a souvenir. Some of the popular Hakka Lei Cha restaurants in Taipei City include Jin Xuan Pai Gu and Yehliu Lei Cha.

Taipei City offers a wide range of unique souvenirs that are perfect for taking back home. From traditional snacks and handicrafts to high-quality liquor and handmade soap, there's something for everyone. Make sure to explore the night markets and specialty shops in Taipei City to find the perfect souvenirs to take back home.

In conclusion, Taipei City offers a diverse range of shopping experiences that cater to every taste and budget. Whether you're looking for luxury shopping malls, trendy boutiques, or traditional souvenirs, Taipei City has something for everyone.

CHAPTER EIGHT

NIGHTLIFE IN TAIPEI CITY

Taipei City is well known for its vibrant nightlife scene, offering something for everyone. If you're into bar hopping, clubbing, live music, or just enjoying a few drinks with friends, Taipei City has it all. The city's nightlife is especially vibrant in the popular districts of Ximending, Zhongxiao Dunhua, and Taipei 101.

Popular Nightlife Districts In Taipei City

Taipei City is a city that never sleeps, and when the sun sets, the city comes alive with its vibrant and diverse nightlife scene. There are several districts that are known for their nightlife in Taipei City, each with its own unique charm and atmosphere.

Ximending
Ximending is a pedestrian-friendly area located in the Wanhua district of Taipei City, and it's one of the most popular nightlife districts in the city. Known as the "Shibuya of Taipei," Ximending is a hub for shopping, entertainment, and youth culture. This district is particularly popular among young

people, and it's a great place to experience the energy and vitality of Taipei's nightlife.

Ximending is a colorful and bustling area that is home to a variety of bars, clubs, karaoke rooms, and street performances. The streets are packed with people, and the atmosphere is lively and fun. It's also a great place to indulge in some late-night snacking, as there are plenty of street food vendors and restaurants in the area.

Some of the popular bars and clubs in Ximending include Luxy, Spark, and Wave Club. These clubs are known for their dance floors, state-of-the-art sound systems, and impressive lineups of local and international DJs. There are also several karaoke rooms in the area, such as Partyworld and Holiday KTV, where you can belt out your favorite tunes with friends.

Zhongxiao Dunhua

Zhongxiao Dunhua is a bustling district located in the Da'an District of Taipei City, and it's another popular nightlife destination. This district is known for its shopping, dining, and entertainment options, and it's particularly popular among the younger crowd.

Zhongxiao Dunhua offers a wide range of bars, clubs, and lounges, catering to different tastes and budgets. Some of the popular bars in the area include Att 4 Fun, Barcode, and Room18. These bars are known for their creative cocktails, live music, and friendly atmosphere. There are also several lounges in the area, such as the Rooftop Bar at eslite hotel, which offers stunning views of Taipei City's skyline.

Taipei 101

Taipei 101 is an iconic skyscraper that dominates Taipei's skyline, and it's home to several upscale bars and lounges. This district offers a more sophisticated nightlife atmosphere compared to other districts, and it's a great place to enjoy a drink with a view.

The top floors of Taipei 101 offer stunning views of Taipei City, and there are several bars and lounges in the area that take advantage of this. Some of the popular bars and lounges in Taipei 101 include the Indulge Acoustic Bar and The Lounge at Grand Hyatt Taipei. These bars are known for their stylish interiors, creative cocktails, and upscale atmosphere.

Shida Night Market

Shida Night Market is a vibrant night market located in the Da'an district of Taipei City. This night market is particularly popular among students from the nearby National Taiwan Normal University, and it's a great place to experience the local food and culture.

The market is lined with food stalls and vendors selling a wide range of Taiwanese snacks and street food, such as stinky tofu, oyster omelets, and bubble tea. There are also several bars and clubs in the area that cater to a younger crowd, such as Revolver and Witch House.

Raohe Night Market
Raohe Night Market is another popular night market located in Taipei City, and it's known for its delicious food and lively atmosphere. This night market is particularly popular among locals, and it's a great place to sample some of Taiwan's most famous dishes.

The market is lined with food stalls selling a wide range of Taiwanese delicacies, such as braised pork rice, fried chicken cutlets, and beef noodle soup. There are also several bars and lounges in the area, such as L'Idiot, which offers a cozy and relaxed atmosphere to enjoy a drink after a long day of exploring the city.

Neihu Technology Park
Neihu Technology Park is a district located in the eastern part of Taipei City, and it's known for its trendy bars and clubs. This district caters to a younger, more affluent crowd, and it's a great place to experience Taipei City's more upscale nightlife scene.

The area is lined with stylish bars and clubs, such as Chess Taipei and Triangle Club, which offer a sophisticated and chic atmosphere. The clubs in Neihu Technology Park are known for their state-of-the-art sound systems, impressive lighting displays, and top-notch DJ lineups.

In conclusion, Taipei City offers several popular nightlife districts, each with its own unique charm and atmosphere. If you're looking for a lively and energetic atmosphere or a more sophisticated and upscale experience, you'll find it in Taipei City's nightlife scene.

Best Bars And Nightclubs In Taipei City

Taipei City's nightlife scene boasts a wide range of bars and nightclubs catering to all tastes and budgets. From underground clubs playing the latest electronic music to upscale bars serving craft cocktails, there's something for everyone. Here are some of the best bars and nightclubs in Taipei City:

Barcode
Located in the upscale Xinyi District, Barcode is a popular nightclub that draws a mix of locals and tourists. The club has a spacious dance floor and features state-of-the-art sound and lighting systems, creating a high-energy atmosphere. Barcode hosts a variety of events and performances, including international DJs and live music acts.

Omni

Omni is a multi-level nightclub located in the bustling Zhongshan District. Each floor of the club offers a different music genre, including EDM, hip-hop, and pop. The club's main room features a giant LED screen and state-of-the-art sound and lighting systems, making it a popular spot for party-goers. Omni hosts events regularly, featuring local and international DJs.

The Pawnshop

Located in the trendy Ximending district, The Pawnshop is a speakeasy-style bar that offers a cozy atmosphere and creative cocktails made with local ingredients. The bar has a vintage decor, and the drinks are served in unique vessels, including teapots and glass beakers. The Pawnshop is known for its excellent drinks and friendly staff, making it a popular spot among locals and tourists alike.

Revolver

Revolver is a live music venue located in the bustling Zhongshan District. The intimate space hosts a variety of local and international acts, from indie bands to electronic DJs. The venue has a casual atmosphere and a small stage, creating an intimate experience for concert-goers. Revolver also serves a selection of craft beers and cocktails.

Marquee

Marquee is an upscale nightclub located in the heart of Taipei's Xinyi District. The club has a modern decor and features a large dance floor, VIP booths, and a terrace with stunning city views. Marquee hosts international DJs and performers regularly and has a dress code policy, so make sure to dress to impress.

Witch House
Witch House is an underground club located in the trendy Ximen area. The club has a gothic decor and plays a variety of electronic music genres, including techno, house, and ambient. Witch House is known for its dark and moody atmosphere and is a favorite spot among music lovers.

In conclusion, Taipei City's nightlife scene offers a variety of bars and nightclubs catering to all tastes and budgets. Whether you're looking for an underground club or an upscale nightclub, Taipei City has it all.

Nighttime Activities In Taipei City

Taipei City is a bustling metropolis that never sleeps, and there are plenty of activities to keep you entertained well into the night. Here are some of the best nighttime activities to enjoy in Taipei City:

Night Markets

Taipei City is known for its vibrant night markets, which are a must-visit for any traveler. The night markets are open until late at night, usually past midnight, and are a great place to sample some of Taiwan's famous street food, shop for souvenirs, and experience the local culture. Some of the most popular night markets in Taipei City are Shilin Night Market, Raohe Street Night Market, and Ningxia Night Market.

Hot Springs

Taipei City is surrounded by natural hot springs, which are a popular destination for locals and tourists alike. The hot springs are open late at night, making them a great option for a relaxing soak after a long day of sightseeing. The most famous hot springs in Taipei City are Beitou Hot Spring, which is located in the Beitou District, and Wulai Hot Spring, which is located in the Wulai District.

Rooftop Bars

Taipei City is home to some of the most impressive rooftop bars in the world, with stunning views of the city skyline. Many of these rooftop bars are open late at night and offer a great atmosphere for socializing and enjoying a drink. Some of the best rooftop bars in Taipei City include Rooftop 18, which is located in the Xinyi District, and the Sky

Bar at W Taipei, which is located in the Xinyi District as well.

Nighttime Hiking
Taipei City is surrounded by mountains and natural trails, which offer a unique experience for night owls. Nighttime hiking is a popular activity in Taipei City, especially during the summer months when the weather is warm. Some of the most popular trails for nighttime hiking in Taipei City are Elephant Mountain Trail and the Four Beasts Trail.

Nighttime City Tours
If you want to see Taipei City's famous landmarks and attractions in a different light, a nighttime city tour is a great option. Many tour companies offer nighttime tours of Taipei City, which include stops at popular landmarks like Taipei 101 and Chiang Kai-Shek Memorial Hall. Some of these tours also include visits to night markets and rooftop bars, making for a fun and memorable night

Karaoke
Karaoke is a popular pastime in Taiwan, and Taipei City has no shortage of karaoke bars that stay open late into the night. Rent a private room with your friends, order some drinks and snacks, and belt out your favorite tunes. Some of the most popular karaoke bars in Taipei City include Cash Box Karaoke and Holiday KTV.

Nightlife Districts

Taipei City has several neighborhoods that are known for their lively nightlife scene. These districts are filled with bars, clubs, and other entertainment venues that stay open late into the night. The most popular nightlife districts in Taipei City include Ximending, which is known for its trendy bars and clubs, and Zhongxiao Dunhua, which is known for its upscale cocktail bars.

Temples at Night

Many of Taipei City's temples are open late into the night, offering a unique opportunity to experience these sacred places in a different light. Baoan Temple, which is located in the Datong District, is particularly popular for nighttime visits, with its ornate decorations and colorful lanterns.

Nighttime Concerts and Events

Taipei City has a vibrant music and arts scene, with many concerts and events taking place at night. From pop concerts to classical performances, there is always something happening in Taipei City's venues. The Taipei Arena and the National Theater and Concert Hall are two of the most popular venues for nighttime events.

Overall, Taipei City has a wealth of nighttime activities to offer travelers, from bustling night markets to relaxing hot springs, lively bars and clubs to serene temples. If you prefer a low-key evening or a night out on the town, there is something for everyone in Taipei City after dark.

CHAPTER NINE

DAY TRIPS FROM TAIPEI CITY

Taipei City is a bustling metropolis that offers a unique mix of modern and traditional attractions. But if you have some extra time, there are plenty of exciting day trips you can take from the city to explore Taiwan's diverse landscapes and cultural heritage.

Popular Day Trips From Taipei City

Taipei City is a bustling metropolis, but just a short distance from the city, there are many exciting day trip options available. These day trips allow visitors to experience Taiwan's diverse landscapes, cultural heritage, and natural beauty. Here are some of the best day trips from Taipei City

Jiufen and Shifen
Jiufen is a small town situated in the mountains of northeastern Taiwan. It was once a gold mining center, but today it is a popular tourist destination

known for its traditional teahouses, narrow alleys, and stunning views of the ocean. Some of the most popular attractions in Jiufen include the Jiufen Old Street, which is lined with shops and restaurants, the A Mei Tea House, which offers panoramic views of the town, and the Jiufen Gold Museum, which showcases the town's gold mining history.

Shifen is another small town located nearby, which is famous for its sky lantern festival. Visitors can purchase a sky lantern and release it into the sky, making a wish as they do so. The town is also home to several other attractions, including the Shifen Waterfall, the Golden Waterfall, and the Yin-Yang Sea.

Yehliu Geopark
Yehliu Geopark is located on Taiwan's northeastern coast and is a unique landscape of bizarre rock formations that have been eroded by the sea over millions of years. The most famous rock formation is the Queen's Head, which resembles the head of a queen wearing a crown. Other highlights include the Mushroom Rocks, the Dragon's Head, and the Fairy Shoe. Visitors can explore the park on foot along the designated paths, and the park also offers guided tours.

Yangmingshan National Park
Yangmingshan National Park is a popular day trip destination that offers visitors a refreshing escape

from the urban jungle. The park is located just a short drive from Taipei City and is famous for its hot springs, hiking trails, and scenic views of Taipei City. Popular attractions include the Yangmingshan Flower Clock, which displays a different flower each season, the Qingtiangang Grassland, which offers sweeping views of the park, and the Xiaoyoukeng volcano, which emits sulfuric fumes.

Wulai

Wulai is a mountain village located just outside of Taipei City, which is known for its hot springs, waterfalls, and aboriginal culture. Visitors can soak in the hot springs, which are said to have healing properties, hike to the Wulai Waterfall, which is over 80 meters high, and learn about the Atayal tribe's customs and traditions at the Wulai Atayal Museum. Other attractions in the area include the Wulai Old Street, which is lined with souvenir shops and restaurants, and the Wulai Skywalk, which offers panoramic views of the surrounding mountains.

Pingxi

Pingxi is a small town located in the mountains of northern Taiwan, which is famous for its sky lantern festival. During the Lantern Festival, visitors can purchase a sky lantern, write their wishes on it, and release it into the sky. Other attractions in the area include the Pingxi Old Street, which is lined with shops and restaurants, the Shifen Waterfall, which is over 20 meters high, and the Jingan Suspension Bridge, which offers stunning views of the surrounding mountains.

When planning a day trip from Taipei City, visitors should consider transportation options, as some attractions may be difficult to reach by public transportation. Some visitors opt to hire a private driver or join a guided tour to make the most of their time. It is also important to bring comfortable walking shoes, sunscreen, and plenty of water, as some attractions may involve a lot of walking or outdoor activities.

In addition to the above mentioned day trip destinations, there are several other options available for visitors to Taipei City. Here are a few additional suggestions:

Danshui

Danshui is a coastal town located just outside of Taipei City, which is famous for its seafood, temples, and historical sites. Visitors can stroll along the Danshui Old Street, which offers a variety of food options and souvenir shops, visit the Fort San Domingo, a former Dutch fort built in the 17th century, and explore the Tamkang University campus, which is known for its beautiful architecture and river views.

Tamsui Fisherman's Wharf

Located at the mouth of the Tamsui River, the Tamsui Fisherman's Wharf is a popular attraction for seafood lovers and sunset watchers. Visitors can enjoy fresh seafood at one of the many restaurants located on the wharf, take a stroll along the waterfront, and watch the sunset over the river.

Beitou Hot Springs

Beitou is a district located in northern Taipei City, which is famous for its hot springs. Visitors can soak in the natural hot springs at one of the many public or private hot spring facilities, explore the Beitou Hot Spring Museum, which showcases the history and culture of hot springs in Taiwan, and take a walk through the Beitou Thermal Valley, which features boiling hot springs and sulfur vents.

National Palace Museum

The National Palace Museum is one of Taiwan's most popular tourist attractions and is home to one of the largest collections of Chinese art and artifacts in the world. Visitors can explore the museum's extensive collection of jade, calligraphy, porcelain, and paintings, and learn about the history and culture of China.

In conclusion, Taipei City is a vibrant and exciting destination, but the surrounding areas offer a variety of day trip options that allow visitors to experience Taiwan's diverse culture, landscapes, and natural beauty. From mountain villages and hot springs to coastal towns and cultural landmarks, there is something for everyone just a short distance from the city. Visitors are encouraged to plan ahead and consider transportation options to make the most of their day trip experience.

Tips For Planning A Day Trip From Taipei City

Decide on your destination: Taipei City is surrounded by many beautiful places that are perfect for a day trip. Some popular options include Jiufen and Shifen, Yehliu Geopark, and Yangmingshan National Park. Do some research and choose the destination that interests you the most.

Check transportation options: Once you've decided on your destination, it's important to check transportation options. Most day trip destinations can be reached by train, bus, or private car. Check the schedules and prices to find the best option for your trip.

Plan your itinerary: Once you know how to get there, plan your itinerary for the day. Research the top attractions in the area and plan out the order in which you'll visit them. Make sure to leave some flexibility in your schedule in case you want to spend more time at a particular location.

Bring essentials: It's important to bring everything you need for a day trip. This might include snacks, water, sunscreen, and comfortable shoes. Check the weather forecast and dress appropriately for the conditions.

Know the cultural norms: If you're visiting a destination outside of Taipei City, it's important to be aware of the local cultural norms. For example, some destinations may have dress codes or require visitors to remove their shoes before entering certain areas.

Consider guided tours: If you're not comfortable navigating on your own, consider taking a guided tour. Many tour operators offer day trips from Taipei City and can provide a knowledgeable guide to show you around.

Check opening times: Before you set out on your day trip, check the opening times of the attractions you want to visit. Some places may have limited hours or be closed on certain days.

Budget for expenses: Day trips can be expensive, especially if you're taking a private car or joining a guided tour. Make sure to budget for expenses like transportation, admission fees, and meals.

By following these tips, you can plan a successful and enjoyable day trip from Taipei City. Just remember to be flexible and open to new experiences, and you're sure to have a great time!

CHAPTER TEN

PRACTICAL INFORMATION FOR TAIPEI CITY

Taipei is a vibrant and welcoming city that attracts visitors from all over the world. To make the most of your trip and avoid any potential issues, it's important to be aware of the local rules and regulations.

Common Rules And Regulations Visitors Should Be Aware Of In Taipei

Here are some of the most important things to keep in mind:

Respect local customs and culture: Taiwan is a country with a rich cultural heritage, and it's important to be respectful of local customs and traditions. This includes things like taking off your shoes before entering a home or temple, bowing as a sign of respect, and avoiding public displays of affection.

Observe the smoking ban: Smoking is banned in most public places in Taipei, including restaurants, bars, and public transport. Be sure to look for designated smoking areas if you need to smoke.

Dispose of trash properly: Taipei is known for its clean streets, and visitors are expected to do their part to keep the city tidy. Be sure to dispose of trash in designated bins and follow recycling guidelines.

Use public transportation responsibly: Taipei has an excellent public transportation system, including buses, subways, and trains. Be sure to follow the rules, such as not eating or drinking on public transport, and giving up your seat to elderly or disabled passengers.

Be aware of scams: While Taipei is generally a safe city, tourists can still be targeted by scams. Common scams include fake taxis, overcharging for goods or services, and pickpocketing. Be sure to use reputable taxis and tour operators, and be wary of anyone who approaches you on the street offering a deal that seems too good to be true.

Dress appropriately: Taipei is a modern and cosmopolitan city, but it's still important to dress modestly in certain settings. For example, it's appropriate to wear more formal attire when visiting a temple or government building, and to cover up at the beach or public pool.

Follow traffic rules: If you plan to drive or rent a scooter in Taipei, be sure to follow local traffic rules. This includes wearing a helmet, driving on the right side of the road, and obeying traffic lights and signs.

Overall, by being aware of these common rules and regulations in Taipei, you can help ensure a smooth and enjoyable trip. Remember to be respectful of local customs and culture, follow the rules, and stay up-to-date on any changes or regulations that may come up during your stay.

Safety And Security

Safety and security are important considerations for any traveler, and Taipei City is generally a safe and welcoming destination. However, it's always a good idea to take precautions and be aware of potential risks.

Crime

Taipei City has a relatively low crime rate compared to other major cities around the world, but petty crimes like pickpocketing and purse snatching can occur, especially in crowded areas like night markets or tourist attractions. To avoid becoming a victim of theft, it's important to keep a close eye on your belongings, especially in crowded areas. Be aware of your surroundings and avoid carrying large amounts of cash or expensive items.

Natural Disasters

Taiwan is located in a region prone to earthquakes and typhoons, which can occur at any time of year. Earthquakes are usually minor and rarely cause serious damage, but it's important to be aware of evacuation procedures and emergency preparedness in case of a major earthquake. Typhoons are more common from May to October, and can cause flooding and landslides. If a typhoon is forecasted during your stay in Taipei City, pay attention to weather updates and follow any evacuation orders or safety guidelines issued by local authorities.

Transportation Safety

Taipei City's public transportation system is generally safe and reliable, but accidents can occur. Be aware of your surroundings and follow safety guidelines when using public transportation. If taking a taxi, ensure that the taxi is licensed and that the driver uses the meter. It's also important to wear a helmet if renting a scooter or bicycle.

Political Protests

Political protests and demonstrations can occur in Taipei City, especially around major government buildings and public squares. If you encounter a protest, avoid the area and do not engage with the protesters. Be aware that protests can sometimes turn violent, and it's important to follow any instructions given by local authorities.

Emergency Services:

In case of an emergency in Taipei City, dial 119 for the fire department or ambulance, or 110 for the police. It's important to have travel insurance that covers emergency medical services and medical evacuation.

Overall, Taipei City is a relatively safe destination for travelers, but it's important to take precautions and be aware of potential risks. By staying alert and following safety guidelines, you can enjoy a safe and enjoyable trip to Taipei City.

Money And Budgeting

Taipei is the capital city of Taiwan, which uses the New Taiwan Dollar (NTD) as its currency. Money and budgeting in Taipei are generally similar to other major cities in the region, with a wide range of options for travelers at different price points.

When it comes to budgeting in Taipei, it's important to keep in mind that the cost of living can vary greatly depending on your lifestyle and the neighborhood you're staying in. Some areas, such as Xinyi and Da'an, are known for their upscale shopping and dining options, while others, like Wanhua and Datong, offer more affordable alternatives.

As a general rule, travelers can expect to spend around NTD 1,500-2,500 per day on food, transportation, and other basic expenses. However, this can vary depending on your preferences and the activities you have planned.

In terms of currency exchange, visitors to Taipei can exchange their home currency for NTD at banks, exchange offices, or ATMs throughout the city. It's generally a good idea to avoid exchanging currency at airports or other tourist areas, as these locations may charge higher fees or offer less favorable exchange rates.

Overall, with a bit of planning and budgeting, visitors to Taipei can enjoy all the city has to offer without breaking the bank.

Currency

The currency used in Taipei City is the New Taiwan Dollar (NTD or TWD). The exchange rate can fluctuate, but at the time of writing, the exchange rate is roughly 1 USD = 30 NTD approximately. It's important to exchange your currency at a reputable exchange bureau or bank to ensure that you receive a fair exchange rate.

Costs in Taipei City

Taipei City can be a relatively affordable destination for travelers, especially compared to other Asian cities like Tokyo or Hong Kong. However, costs can vary depending on your travel style and preferences. On average, a budget traveler can expect to spend around NT$1,000-1,500 ($35-55 USD) per day on food, transportation, and accommodation. Mid-range travelers can expect to spend around NT$2,000-3,000 ($70-105 USD) per day, while luxury travelers can expect to spend upwards of NT$5,000 ($175 USD) per day.

Accommodation Costs

Accommodation costs can vary depending on the type of accommodation you choose and its location. Hostels and budget hotels can cost as little as NT$500-800 ($18-28 USD) per night, while mid-range hotels can cost around NT$1,500-3,000 ($53-105 USD) per night. Luxury hotels can cost upwards of NT$5,000 ($175 USD) per night. It's worth noting that accommodation prices can be higher during peak travel seasons or during major events like the Taipei Lantern Festival or the Taipei International Food Expo.

Food and Drink Costs

Taipei City is known for its delicious and affordable street food, which can cost as little as NT$30-50 ($1-2 USD) per dish. Dining at a mid-range restaurant can cost around NT$200-400 ($7-14

USD) per meal, while dining at a high-end restaurant can cost upwards of NT$1,000 ($35 USD) per meal. It's worth noting that tipping is not expected in restaurants in Taipei City.

Transportation Costs
As mentioned in the Transportation section, the MRT is the most convenient and affordable way to get around Taipei City, with fares starting at NT$20 ($0.70 USD). A reloadable EasyCard can be used on all modes of public transportation and even at some convenience stores, and can save you money in the long run. Taxis are also relatively affordable, with fares starting at NT$70 ($2.50 USD) for the first 1.25 km.

Other Costs:
Other costs to consider when budgeting for Taipei City include admission fees to tourist attractions (which can range from free to NT$500 ($18 USD) or more), shopping expenses, and any day trips or excursions outside of the city.

Payment Methods
Credit cards are widely accepted in Taipei City, especially in major tourist areas and hotels. However, it's always a good idea to carry some cash for small transactions and to shop at local markets and street vendors. ATMs are widely available throughout the city, and many accept foreign cards. It's important to notify your bank or credit card

company before traveling to ensure that your cards will work abroad.

Overall, budgeting for Taipei City can be relatively straightforward, but it's important to consider your travel style and preferences when planning your budget. By understanding the costs associated with accommodation, food and drink, transportation, and other expenses, you can plan a budget that suits your needs and allows you to make the most of your time in Taipei City.

Taipei City can be a relatively affordable destination for travelers, but costs can vary depending on your travel style and preferences. On average, a budget traveler can expect to spend around NT$1,000-1,500 ($35-55 USD) per day on food, transportation, and accommodation. Mid-range travelers can expect to spend around NT$2,000-3,000 ($70-105 USD) per day, while luxury travelers can expect to spend upwards of NT$5,000 ($175 USD) per day. It's important to note that credit cards are widely accepted in Taipei City, but it's always a good idea to carry some cash for small transactions.

Useful Phrases In Mandarin

While many locals in Taipei City speak English, learning a few basic phrases in Mandarin can go a long way in making connections with locals and enhancing your experience. Here are a few essential phrases to know:

- Thank you: Xiè xiè (pronounced "sheh sheh")

- Hello: Nǐ hǎo (pronounced "nee how")

- I don't understand: Wǒ bù dǒng (pronounced "woh boo dong")

- Can you speak English? Nǐ huì shuō yīngyǔ ma? (pronounced "nee hway shwoh ying yoo ma?")

- How much is this? Zhè ge duōshǎo qián? (pronounced "jeh guh dwoh shaow chyen?")

- Where is the bathroom? Xǐshǒujiān zài nǎlǐ? (pronounced "sheh shoh jyen zye naa lee?")

- Do you have...? Nǐ yǒu méiyǒu...? (pronounced "nee yo may yo?")

- Yes: Shì (pronounced "shir")

- No: Bù shì (pronounced "boo shir")

- For example: Nǐ yǒu méiyǒu wàimào xiàn? (Do you have a foreign currency exchange?)

- Excuse me, where is...? Duì bù qǐ, ...zài nǎlǐ? (pronounced "dway boo chee, ...zye naa lee?")

- For example: Duì bù qǐ, Táiběi 101 zài nǎlǐ? (Excuse me, where is Taipei 101?)

- I would like...: Wǒ xiǎng yào... (pronounced "woh shyang yao...")

- For example: Wǒ xiǎng yào yī bēi kāfēi. (I would like a cup of coffee.)
- That's too expensive: Tài guì le (pronounced "tie gway luh")

- Can you help me? Nǐ néng bāng wǒ ma? (pronounced "nee nung bung woh ma?")

- I'm sorry: Duì bù qǐ (pronounced "dway boo chee")

Remember, even if your Mandarin pronunciation isn't perfect, locals will appreciate your effort to communicate in their language. Additionally, using basic phrases like "hello" and "thank you" can help you make a positive impression and build connections with locals.

Useful Website And Resources

Here's a comprehensive list of useful websites and resources that tourists/travelers should be aware of in Taipei:

Taiwan Tourism Bureau: This is the official website of the Taiwan Tourism Bureau, which offers a wealth of information about travel and tourism in Taiwan. Visitors can find information on local attractions, events, accommodations, and transportation options.

Taipei City Government Tourism and Travel: The Taipei City Government's tourism and travel website provides a wealth of information on local attractions, events, and accommodations, as well as travel tips and guides for tourists.

Taipei Metro: The Taipei Metro is a rapid transit system that covers much of the city, making it a convenient and affordable way to get around. The metro's website provides maps, schedules, and fare information, as well as real-time updates on train arrivals and departures.

Taiwan High Speed Rail: The Taiwan High Speed Rail is a high-speed train system that connects Taipei with other major cities in Taiwan. The website provides schedules, fares, and booking information, as well as travel tips and guides for tourists.

Taipei Fun Pass: The Taipei Fun Pass is a tourist pass that offers discounts on local attractions, restaurants, and transportation options. The website provides information on the different types of passes available, as well as where to purchase them and how to use them.

Taipei Travel Net: Taipei Travel Net is a website that offers information on local accommodations, restaurants, and attractions, as well as travel guides and tips for tourists.

Taiwan Weather Bureau: The Taiwan Weather Bureau provides up-to-date weather forecasts and typhoon warnings for Taipei and other cities in Taiwan. This is particularly useful for tourists who are planning outdoor activities or day trips.

Yelp Taipei: Yelp Taipei is a popular review site that provides information on local restaurants, bars, and attractions, as well as user reviews and ratings.

Google Maps: Google Maps is a useful tool for navigating Taipei and finding local attractions and restaurants. It also provides real-time traffic updates and directions for walking, driving, or taking public transportation.

Translation Apps: Translation apps are useful tools you can use to communicate with the local to bridge the communication gap.

Overall, these websites and resources can help tourists/travelers plan their trip to Taipei, navigate the city, and make the most of their time in Taiwan.

CHAPTER ELEVEN

MY 19 TO DO LIST IN TAIPEI CITY FOR AN UNFORGETTABLE EXPERIENCE AS A TOURIST/TRAVELLER

Here are 19 things to do in Taipei City for an unforgettable experience as a tourist/traveler

1. **Taipei 101:** Taipei 101 is a must-see landmark in Taipei City. It was once the tallest building in the world and offers stunning panoramic views of the city from its observation deck on the 89th floor. The tower also houses luxury shops, restaurants, and cafes.

2. **National Palace Museum:** The National Palace Museum is a world-renowned museum that houses a vast collection of Chinese art and artifacts. It has over 700,000 items, including paintings, ceramics, jade, and bronze objects. Some of the museum's most famous exhibits include the Jadeite Cabbage and the Meat-shaped Stone.

3. **Wanhua:** Wanhua is Taipei City's oldest district and is rich in history and culture. The district is home to the famous Longshan Temple, which was built in the 18th century and is dedicated to Guanyin, the Buddhist goddess of mercy. Visitors can also explore the traditional markets and street food stalls in the area.

4. **Beitou Hot Springs:** Beitou Hot Springs is a popular destination for locals and tourists alike. The natural geothermal waters are rich in minerals and are said to have therapeutic properties. Visitors can soak in the hot springs at various public and private bathhouses in the area.

5. **Ximending:** Ximending is a vibrant and trendy shopping district that is popular among young people. The area is known for its unique shops, boutiques, and night markets. It is also a hub for Taiwanese street fashion and is home to many theaters and performance venues.

6. **Taipei Zoo:** The Taipei Zoo is home to over 4,000 animals from over 400 species, including giant pandas, koalas, and penguins. Visitors can also explore the zoo's ecological

exhibits and learn about conservation efforts in Taiwan.

7. **Xinyi District:** The Xinyi District is a modern and upscale area that is home to luxury hotels, high-end shops, and trendy restaurants and bars. It is also known for its impressive architecture, including the Taipei 101 tower and the Taipei City Government building.

8. **Dihua Street:** Dihua Street is a historic market that dates back to the Qing Dynasty. The street is lined with traditional shops selling goods such as Chinese medicine, dried foods, and local delicacies. Visitors can also explore the street's historic buildings and temples.

9. **Sun Yat-sen Memorial Hall:** The Sun Yat-sen Memorial Hall is a tribute to the father of modern China, who led the revolution that overthrew the Qing Dynasty. The memorial hall houses exhibits on Sun Yat-sen's life and legacy and features a large plaza that is often used for events and ceremonies.

10. **Jiufen:** Jiufen is a mountain village located about an hour's drive from Taipei City. The village is known for its stunning views of the ocean and the traditional architecture of

its buildings. Visitors can also explore the many shops and tea houses in the area.

11. **Night Market Food Tour:** Taipei City is known for its vibrant night markets, which offer a wide variety of street food and snacks. A night market food tour is a great way to try out some of the most popular and delicious Taiwanese dishes, such as stinky tofu, oyster omelet, and bubble tea.

12. **Taipei Fine Arts Museum:** The Taipei Fine Arts Museum is a contemporary art museum that features works by both Taiwanese and international artists. The museum hosts a wide variety of exhibits and events throughout the year.

13. **Huashan 1914 Creative Park:** The Huashan 1914 Creative Park is a unique arts and culture complex that features exhibitions, performances, and workshops. The park was once a winery and has been transformed into a creative space that showcases both local and international art and culture.

14. **Chiang Kai-shek Memorial Hall:** The Chiang Kai-shek Memorial Hall is a national monument dedicated to the former president of the Republic of China. The memorial hall features a large statue of Chiang

Kai-shek and houses a museum that displays artifacts related to his life and legacy.

15. **Elephant Mountain:** Elephant Mountain is a popular hiking destination in Taipei City that offers breathtaking views of the city skyline. The hike takes about 20-30 minutes and is relatively easy, making it accessible to hikers of all levels.

16. **Shilin Night Market:** The Shilin Night Market is one of the most famous night markets in Taipei City. It is known for its wide variety of food stalls and vendors selling everything from clothing to souvenirs. Visitors can also enjoy carnival games and performances in the area.

17. **Maokong Gondola:** The Maokong Gondola is a cable car that takes visitors on a scenic ride up to the mountainside tea plantations in Maokong. The ride offers stunning views of Taipei City and the surrounding mountains.

18. **Taipei City Mall:** The Taipei City Mall is an underground shopping complex that spans over 20 kilometers. The mall is home to over 1000 shops and vendors selling everything from clothing to electronics.

19. **National Revolutionary Martyrs' Shrine:** The National Revolutionary Martyrs' Shrine is a monument dedicated to the soldiers who died fighting for Taiwan's independence. The shrine features an impressive gate, a main hall, and a large courtyard that is used for ceremonial events.

Overall, Taipei City offers a wide range of activities and experiences for visitors to enjoy. From exploring the city's rich history and culture to indulging in its vibrant food and shopping scenes, there is something for everyone in this bustling metropolis.

CONCLUSION

Taipei City is the capital city of Taiwan and is one of the most visited destinations in Asia. It is a city that offers a perfect blend of old and new with modern skyscrapers, traditional temples, museums, and night markets that showcase its rich cultural heritage. It is also known for its culinary delights and street food that has gained worldwide recognition.

Getting to Taipei City is easy with its well-connected international airport, high-speed rail, and excellent public transportation system. Visitors can choose from a wide range of accommodation options including luxury hotels, hostels, and guesthouses located in popular areas of the city.

One of the top tourist attractions in Taipei City is the National Palace Museum that houses a vast collection of ancient Chinese art and artifacts. Taipei 101, formerly the world's tallest building, is also a must-visit landmark offering panoramic views of the city. Other notable tourist attractions include the Chiang Kai-Shek Memorial Hall, Taipei Zoo, and Longshan Temple.

Visitors can also explore the hidden gems of Taipei City, including lesser-known temples, traditional markets, and unique neighborhoods that offer a glimpse into the local way of life. Night markets like Shilin and Raohe offer an opportunity to sample Taiwanese street food and indulge in shopping.

Taipei City is a foodie's paradise with a wide range of Taiwanese cuisine to suit all tastes. Some of the must-try dishes include bubble tea, beef noodle soup, and stinky tofu. Taipei City's night markets are also famous for their street food, including oyster omelets, fried chicken, and grilled squid.

Shopping in Taipei City is a popular activity with several shopping districts and malls that cater to different budgets and tastes. Visitors can find everything from luxury brands to local handicrafts and souvenirs.

Taipei City's nightlife scene is vibrant and diverse with several bars, nightclubs, and entertainment venues catering to different interests. Popular nightlife districts include Xinyi, Zhongxiao Dunhua, and Taipei Main Station.

Finally, visitors can take day trips from Taipei City to explore the beautiful natural landscapes surrounding the city. Jiufen and Shifen are popular destinations for their picturesque towns and stunning waterfalls, while Yangmingshan National Park offers hiking trails, hot springs, and scenic views of Taipei City.

Taipei City is a fascinating and unique destination that offers something for everyone. From its rich cultural heritage to its culinary delights and natural beauty, Taipei City is a must-visit destination for travelers looking to explore Asia.

ON A FINAL NOTE

The information provided in this travel guide is based on research and personal experience at the time of writing. However, travel conditions and regulations can change quickly and without notice. Therefore, readers are advised to do their own research and exercise their own judgment before making travel plans or decisions. The author and publisher of this travel guide are not responsible for any inaccuracies or omissions, nor for any damages or losses that may result from following the information provided in this guide.

Thank you for choosing this TAIPEI CITY TRAVEL GUIDE, and bon voyage!

Made in the USA
Monee, IL
24 April 2023

32371548R00087

$12.99